W9-BAF-222

OPPOSING
VIEWPOINTS®
SERIES

Feminism

Other Books of Related Interest

Opposing Viewpoints Series

Identity Politics
Violent Video Games and Society
Women's Health
Working Women

At Issue Series

Campus Sexual Violence
Gender Politics
Reproductive Rights
Sexual Assault and the Military

Current Controversies Series

Abortion
LGBTQ Rights
Microaggressions, Safe Spaces, and Trigger Warnings
Political Correctness

> "Congress shall make no law ... abridging the freedom of speech, or of the press."

First Amendment to the US Constitution

The basic foundation of our democracy is the First Amendment guarantee of freedom of expression. The Opposing Viewpoints series is dedicated to the concept of this basic freedom and the idea that it is more important to practice it than to enshrine it.

OPPOSING
VIEWPOINTS®
SERIES

| Feminism

Avery Elizabeth Hurt, Book Editor

GREENHAVEN
PUBLISHING

Published in 2019 by Greenhaven Publishing, LLC
353 3rd Avenue, Suite 255, New York, NY 10010

Cover image: Mario Tama/Getty Images

Library of Congress Cataloging-in-Publication Data

Names: Hurt, Avery Elizabeth, editor.
Title: Feminism / Avery Elizabeth Hurt, book editor.
Description: New York : Greenhaven Publishing, [2019] | Series: Opposing
  viewpoints | Includes bibliographical references and index. | Audience: Grades 9–12.
Identifiers: LCCN 2018003660| ISBN 9781534502918 (library bound) | ISBN
  9781534502925 (pbk.)
Subjects: LCSH: Feminism—Juvenile literature.
Classification: LCC HQ1150 .F4524 2019 | DDC 305.42—dc23
LC record available at https://lccn.loc.gov/2018003660

Manufactured in the United States of America

Website: http://greenhavenpublishing.com

Contents

Chapter 3: Has Feminism Changed Things for Women?

Chapter 4: What Is Feminism Today?

The Importance of Opposing Viewpoints

Perhaps every generation experiences a period in time in which the populace seems especially polarized, starkly divided on the important issues of the day and gravitating toward the far ends of the political spectrum and away from a consensus-facilitating middle ground. The world that today's students are growing up in and that they will soon enter into as active and engaged citizens is deeply fragmented in just this way. Issues relating to terrorism, immigration, women's rights, minority rights, race relations, health care, taxation, wealth and poverty, the environment, policing, military intervention, the proper role of government—in some ways, perennial issues that are freshly and uniquely urgent and vital with each new generation—are currently roiling the world.

If we are to foster a knowledgeable, responsible, active, and engaged citizenry among today's youth, we must provide them with the intellectual, interpretive, and critical-thinking tools and experience necessary to make sense of the world around them and of the all-important debates and arguments that inform it. After all, the outcome of these debates will in large measure determine the future course, prospects, and outcomes of the world and its peoples, particularly its youth. If they are to become successful members of society and productive and informed citizens, students need to learn how to evaluate the strengths and weaknesses of someone else's arguments, how to sift fact from opinion and fallacy, and how to test the relative merits and validity of their own opinions against the known facts and the best possible available information. The landmark series Opposing Viewpoints has been providing students with just such critical-thinking skills and exposure to the debates surrounding society's most urgent contemporary issues for many years, and it continues to serve this essential role with undiminished commitment, care, and rigor.

The key to the series's success in achieving its goal of sharpening students' critical-thinking and analytic skills resides in its title—

Opposing Viewpoints. In every intriguing, compelling, and engaging volume of this series, readers are presented with the widest possible spectrum of distinct viewpoints, expert opinions, and informed argumentation and commentary, supplied by some of today's leading academics, thinkers, analysts, politicians, policy makers, economists, activists, change agents, and advocates. Every opinion and argument anthologized here is presented objectively and accorded respect. There is no editorializing in any introductory text or in the arrangement and order of the pieces. No piece is included as a "straw man," an easy ideological target for cheap point-scoring. As wide and inclusive a range of viewpoints as possible is offered, with no privileging of one particular political ideology or cultural perspective over another. It is left to each individual reader to evaluate the relative merits of each argument— as he or she sees it, and with the use of ever-growing critical-thinking skills—and grapple with his or her own assumptions, beliefs, and perspectives to determine how convincing or successful any given argument is and how the reader's own stance on the issue may be modified or altered in response to it.

This process is facilitated and supported by volume, chapter, and selection introductions that provide readers with the essential context they need to begin engaging with the spotlighted issues, with the debates surrounding them, and with their own perhaps shifting or nascent opinions on them. In addition, guided reading and discussion questions encourage readers to determine the authors' point of view and purpose, interrogate and analyze the various arguments and their rhetoric and structure, evaluate the arguments' strengths and weaknesses, test their claims against available facts and evidence, judge the validity of the reasoning, and bring into clearer, sharper focus the reader's own beliefs and conclusions and how they may differ from or align with those in the collection or those of their classmates.

Research has shown that reading comprehension skills improve dramatically when students are provided with compelling, intriguing, and relevant "discussable" texts. The subject matter of these collections could not be more compelling, intriguing, or urgently relevant to today's students and the world they are poised to inherit. The anthologized articles and the reading and discussion questions that are included with them also provide the basis for stimulating, lively, and passionate classroom debates. Students who are compelled to anticipate objections to their own argument and identify the flaws in those of an opponent read more carefully, think more critically, and steep themselves in relevant context, facts, and information more thoroughly. In short, using discussable text of the kind provided by every single volume in the Opposing Viewpoints series encourages close reading, facilitates reading comprehension, fosters research, strengthens critical thinking, and greatly enlivens and energizes classroom discussion and participation. The entire learning process is deepened, extended, and strengthened.

For all of these reasons, Opposing Viewpoints continues to be exactly the right resource at exactly the right time—when we most need to provide readers with the critical-thinking tools and skills that will not only serve them well in school but also in their careers and their daily lives as decision-making family members, community members, and citizens. This series encourages respectful engagement with and analysis of opposing viewpoints and fosters a resulting increase in the strength and rigor of one's own opinions and stances. As such, it helps make readers "future ready," and that readiness will pay rich dividends for the readers themselves, for the citizenry, for our society, and for the world at large.

Introduction

> "I raise up my voice—not so I can
> shout, but so that those without a
> voice can be heard ... we cannot
> succeed when half of us are
> held back."
>
> —Malala Yousafzai,
> I Am Malala, 2013.

Every December, Merriam-Webster.com, publishes a list of words of the year. For the year 2017, sitting at the top of the list was "feminism."

Merriam-Webster's list is based on the number of "lookups" during the year—that is, how many times people have grabbed their phones or computers and zipped over to the Merriam-Webster site to find the meaning of the word. So why was 2017 such a big year for feminism? After all, most of us know what it means, don't we? Well, maybe not. It's complicated.

Some scholars trace feminism back to the Greek poet Sappho and her legendary school for women on the isle of Lesbos. But a serious movement focused on achieving rights for women had to wait until very nearly the twentieth century. What is now called the first wave of feminism took place between the nineteenth and early twentieth century when women began to campaign for the right to vote. The 1960s and 1970s saw the second wave, when the movement began to focus more on reproductive rights and economic equality. The Third Wave is happening now. As we shall see in the coming chapters, it has expanded to cover a great deal more than just political and economic equality.

Though the third wave of feminism is generally thought to have begun in the 1990s, the 2016 US presidential election gave it renewed energy and motivation—and brought to the cause many young women who might not otherwise have been active. (Some people saw this as the beginning of a fourth wave.) During his presidential campaign, Donald Trump made no secret of his misogynist tendencies. Then, shortly before the election, a videotape emerged showing the candidate bragging about how, owing to his celebrity status as a game-show host, he could get away with assaulting women, and often did. Many women and men, whether or not they called themselves feminists, were outraged.

The year 2017 began with millions of women all over the United States taking to the streets the day after Trump's inauguration, wearing bright pink cat-eared "pussy" hats to express their disapproval of the newly-elected President, Donald Trump. When the numbers were finally tallied, it was said to be the largest protest in US history.

However, as united in opposition to Trump as the marchers were then, the movement is not without fissures. Third-wave feminism has been beset with conflicts. Pro-life feminists often feel excluded, and many people are disturbed that the women's movement seems to be driven primarily by the concerns and personalities of women with white skin and white collars. Advertising often seems to have co-opted the cause to sell products, reducing a powerful political movement to slogans on T-shirts and hashtags on Twitter. Defining the word "feminism" has suddenly become a lot more difficult.

Nonetheless, the basics haven't changed. As the author of a viewpoint in this resource put it, "In order to be considered a feminist, you only need to be on board with one idea: All humans, male and female, should have equal political, economic and social rights." The rest of the authors here deal with various devils in the details.

The very strange year that was 2017 ended with what came to be known as the #metoo movement, a seismic shift in the nation's attitudes about sexual improprieties that occurred as many women came forward to share their stories of harassment and outright assault by bosses and colleagues. A truly astonishing roll call of powerful men, from movie moguls to politicians to media executives, were accused of and often forced to admit to varying degrees of sexual assault and harassment.

How much things will change for women because of these events remains to be seen. But they certainly brought many of the issues of feminism back to the forefront of the public conversation. #Metoo quickly came to mean more than, "I was also sexually abused." It has a subtext that fairly shouts, "I, too, want fair and equal treatment. Respect. A voice." And that voice doesn't seem to be fading.

In chapters titled "Is Feminism Still Relevant?" "Why Are There So Few Women Leaders?" "Has Feminism Changed Things for Women?" and "What Is Feminism Today?" the viewpoints in *Opposing Viewpoints: Feminism* examine feminism from a variety of perspectives, but one thing they all demonstrate is that we don't really need to define the movement to know it when we see it. A sea of two million women in pink-knitted hats makes a statement of its own.

OPPOSING
VIEWPOINTS®
SERIES

CHAPTER 1

Is Feminism Still Relevant?

Chapter Preface

Before launching into a debate about feminism, it might be prudent to define the subject and examine whether or not the movement is even relevant any longer. Many have argued that the election of Donald Trump—a man who more or less confessed on camera to assaulting women—re-energized the women's movement. And indeed, events like the huge women's march on Washington the day after his inauguration and subsequent activism on the part of feminists seem to support that view.

However, in recent years, the women's movement has splintered into so many factions and created so much controversy that many women, even those who wholeheartedly support gender equality, are hesitant to align themselves with the movement, and are unwilling to call themselves feminists. It can be argued that the word feminism no longer has any meaning, that if the aims of the movement are to be achieved, feminists need to, paradoxically, abandon not only the terminology, but some of their tactics as well.

At the same time, others complain that all too many people—especially celebrities and young women—have lost sight of the most important aims of the movement. Rather than going off the rails, the movement had become diluted and turned into a marketing tool with the aims of selling products rather than achieving social change. The people most in need of the changes feminism seeks to bring about are poor women and women of color. Yet they are for the most part ignored by many of feminism's leaders.

The viewpoints in this chapter take a variety of perspectives on what feminism is, what it has become, and, if it is still necessary, what issues it needs to address. But first, we start will an explanation of the many faces of feminism.

> "*[Feminism] provides a structural framework for making sense of thorny personal issues, and it offers a shared commitment to resolve these issues.*"

Feminism Has Many Faces

Rachel Fudge

In the following excerpted viewpoint, Rachel Fudge argues that, if you think you know what feminism is, and what feminists believe, you have a lot to learn. Fudge discusses the many different ideologies that come under the rubric of feminism. While this section closes with the statement that particular labels and objectives are less important than the common goal of making sure that one's civil or personal liberties are not violated because of one's gender, Fudge gives a detailed accounting of what many different people mean when they say they are feminists. Fudge is a writer and editor in the San Francisco Bay area.

"Everything You Always Wanted to Know About Feminism But Were Afraid to Ask," by Rachel Fudge as published by Bitch Media on November 30, 2005. Reprinted by permission.

As you read, consider the following questions:

1. Do you think having so many different takes on the aims of feminism would harm or help the cause of women?
2. How does Fudge define the word "liberal"? Is that different from what you've come to think of the word as meaning?
3. Do you think these labels are useful? Why or why not?

You wouldn't know it from the blanket terms used to talk about feminism, but the movement's rich history (and current practice) encompasses a slew of ideologies, offshoots, and internal disagreements: radical feminism, cultural feminism, liberal feminism, antiporn feminism, pro-sex feminism, third-wave feminism, womanism—but what does it all mean? A brief primer on the etiology of feminism is sorely needed. The following is hardly exhaustive, and only barely objective, and I must mention that many of the nuances and linguistic turns are still up for debate by and among feminists. So leave your preconceptions behind and join me in this exciting exploration of one of life's most basic urges: feminism.

Liberal Feminism, AKA Just Plain Feminism

Unless you're reading academic treatises about the history or political philosophies of feminism, you almost never hear the term "liberal feminism"—despite the fact that it's the most accurate descriptor for almost all of the mainstream institutional and legislative feminism at work in the United States today. Want to level the playing field? Break the glass ceiling? Make room for women at the table of power? Then you're espousing liberal feminism. Campaigns for legislative-based gender equity—from the ERA to Title IX to Roe v. Wade to the Violence Against Women Act to landmark sexual-harassment suits like the one detailed in the recent film *North Country*—all arise out of liberal feminism.

The "liberal" part refers not to today's muddled characterizations of Democrats, progressives, or granolas in general but rather to the 300-year-old political philosophy detailing the natural rights of "man": inalienable rights to government, property, the development of powers, and gratification of desire—in other words, life, liberty, the pursuit of happiness, and the right to vote and to shop.

Today, liberal feminism is at work in the countless local, state, and federal bills that attempt to codify the seemingly no-duh stance that gender should not be a factor in education, employment, housing, or anything else.

Suffrage

The centuries-long fight for women's right to vote was not just about ballot-casting, but about securing women's right to participate as full citizens: to hold property, keep their own wages, have guardianship of their children, and, yes, vote. While these rights are all direct outgrowths of classic liberalism, it's worth noting that when, in the mid-1800s, Elizabeth Cady Stanton argued that suffrage must be added to the platform of the nascent women's rights campaign, she was considered by many of her supporters—let alone her detractors—to be ridiculous, if not dangerously radical. And subsequent suffrage campaigners like Alice Paul truly were militant activists, engaging in acts of civil disobedience to the disdain of more conservative suffragists like Carrie Chapman Catt, whose tactics centered more on discreet but steady lobbying. (This time is also known retrospectively as the first wave of feminism.)

Equal Rights Amendment (ERA)

The liberal feminist holy grail. In one stroke, it declares: "Equality of rights under the law shall not be denied or abridged by the United States or by any state on account of sex." First drafted and proposed by Alice Paul and the National Woman's Party in 1923, the ERA was introduced in every session of Congress until it finally passed in 1972, thanks to the nationwide energy generated by second wave feminism. Born out of women's frustrations at the sexism of their male comrades in the antiwar, student left, and civil rights movements in the late '60s, the women's liberation movement (which came to be known as second-wave feminism) encompassed a range of strategies, from NOW-style liberal feminism to smash-the-patriarchy radical feminism. sending it to the states for ratification. In one year, 22 of the required 38 states had ratified it, but then the campaign slowed down. Despite an extension—and thanks to the admittedly impressive (if unhinged) efforts of Phyllis Schlafly, whose STOP ERA campaign played on public fears of women getting drafted and unisex bathrooms—it fizzled out. The ERA, or a differently named version of it, has been introduced—unsuccessfully—in every subsequent Congress. So ladies, the next time you hear someone say, "Didn't all that feminist stuff get solved in the '80s?" remind them that, in the eyes of the US Constitution, women are still not equal to men.

National Organization for Women (NOW)

The liberal feminist organization of record was established in 1966 by Betty Friedan, among others, to "take action to bring women into full participation in the mainstream of American society now, exercising all privileges and responsibilities thereof in truly equal partnership with men." Its mission statement today has evolved into a less classically liberal position: "NOW is dedicated to making legal, political, social and economic change in our society in order to achieve our goal, which is to eliminate sexism and end all oppression."

Womanism; Black Feminism

Black women like Cellestine Ware, Pauli Murray, and Shirley Chisholm, to name just a few, were an integral part of the early women's liberation movement, especially the branches that arose out of women's experiences in the civil rights movement. But early efforts to characterize a universal female experience were largely informed by a white American middle-class perspective, and were thus problematic. The National Black Feminist Organization, created in 1973, is one of the groups that were established to broaden the black liberation struggle to include women's concerns and to stake black women's claim to the women's liberation movement.

Black feminists have been joined by Chicana feminists like Gloria Anzuldúa and Cherríe Moraga and other women of color to broaden the scope of feminism beyond a white middle-class perspective and to explore the intersections of ethnicity, race, class, and gender.

Equity Feminism

This is a sly attempt by antifeminist "feminists"—such as Christina Hoff Sommers, author of *Who Stole Feminism?* (1994), and the freaky neocon think tank called the Independent Women's Forum—to appeal to the sentient public that by and large agrees with concepts like equal pay for equal work without actually acknowledging that sexism still exists. (Who can argue with equity?) But as wielded by Hoff Sommers, the IWF, and others, it's really just another word for antifeminism, unchecked capitalism, corporate welfare, and neoconservatism.

Radical Feminism

Part 1: Definition

Radical feminism arose in the late 1960s as a political movement that identified the oppression of women, as a sex-based class or caste, as the most pernicious oppression of them all. The "radical" part came from its proponents' background in the student left, civil rights, and antiwar movements, and was coupled with "feminist" to formulate a radical approach to women's liberation. Radical feminists wanted not for women to share power with men but to abolish the notion of power itself—starting with the sex roles that establish power relations between genders. They led direct actions like the 1968 protest against the Miss America pageant and a sit-in at *Ladies' Home Journal.*

[…]

(Some radical feminists, in looking at the overwhelming reach of patriarchy, advocated female separatism as an antidote—helping create the enduring myth that feminists are man-haters.)

[…]

More moderate folks who aren't well versed in feminist history or theory tend to associate any outspoken expression of feminist leanings as "radical," so that any instance of speaking up, even softly, becomes associated with the word. Valerie Solanas, the author of the satiric 1967 S.C.U.M. Manifesto that advocated destroying "the male sex" (along with capitalism) is frequently labeled a radical feminist, despite the fact that she was never a part of any organized feminist group, and her public feminist efforts were limited to the manifesto. At the other end of the spectrum, we have the bubblegum-pink "radical feminist" T-shirt sold by the Feminist Majority Foundation, which, while hardly the most egregious offense, still largely misses the point: Radical feminism has a rich history and complex etiology of its own that goes beyond Grrrr! I'm a feisty femme(inist) and you better not mess with me!

[…]

Third-Wave Feminism

When the media takes a moment off from ponderously declaring feminism dead or irrelevant to have a look around at contemporary feminists, all it seems to find are third-wavers: If you're under 40 and you're a feminist, then you're a third-wave feminist— regardless of your politics.

While the first wave of feminism (the campaign for women's suffrage) spanned some 150 years, the second wave was allotted less than a quarter-century before being declared "over" by the mainstream media, most notably by *Time*'s 1989 cover story (careful readers will note that this one was a full nine years before their even more infamous 1998 "Is Feminism Dead?" cover). Thus, in 1989, when NOW president Patricia Ireland declared that, in response to increasing federal and state restrictions on abortion, a "third wave is coming," she was acknowledging both the effect of the decade-long backlash (soon to be limned by Susan Faludi in her 1991 book of the same name) in dampening the public face of feminism and the growing activism by young, college-age women. In 1992, Rebecca Walker and Shannon Liss formed the Third Wave Direct Action Corporation (which became the Third Wave Foundation) to mobilize young people—especially young women—to become politically active; its commitment to a multiracial, multigender, and multiclass organizing effort is a hallmark of the best of third-wave activism.

[…]

Today, "third-wave feminism" is often used to describe a kind of companionable, man-friendly, pro-sex, pro–femininity-if-you-want-it feminism that reflects the successes of the second wave's struggle for equal footing. Although third-wave feminists are engaged in a wide variety of grassroots political organizing (from voter-registration drives to campaigns to save abortion rights), much of the ink spilled on the third wave from both the mainstream press and feminist anthologies paints a picture of a generation that is more interested in self-determination and individual decisions than in understanding the political impact of them.

Girlie Feminism

Jennifer Baumgardner and Amy Richards coined this term in their 2000 book *Manifesta: Young Women, Feminism, and the Future* to describe the pro-femininity line of young feminists, most notably expressed by *Bust*. The reclamation of makeup and other girly accoutrements, and the validation of traditionally female activities like cooking, crafting, and talking about sex, they concluded, is a valid way to express the desire for equality—valuing the inherently female aspects of life, rather than trying to erase them. Unfortunately, the tenets of girlie feminism—that women's work is valuable; that crafts are a powerful link to female history; that sexual experimentation is a potent means of feminist expression—have been easily co-opted by market forces and, in many cases, diluted by the resulting slew of consumer products.

Pro-Sex Feminism

The pro-sex line of feminism was born out of the '80s porn wars, in reaction to both the feminist antiporn crusades and the sexual repression of the early Reagan years, and owes its name to a *Village Voice* article by Ellen Willis titled "Lust Horizons: Is the Women's Movement Pro-Sex?" What began as an exploration of the power politics of sexuality by women like Willis, Gayle Rubin, and Betty Dodson evolved during the '90s into an explicit sex-positive approach to feminism. (In a distinct nod to the complicated identity of radical feminism, some sex-positive feminists also use the term "sex radical" to describe themselves.) Proponents run the gamut from theorists like bell hooks and Patrick Califia to erotica-and-criticism writers like Susie Bright and Rachel Kramer Bussel to performance artists like Annie Sprinkle.

I'm Not a Feminist But … Feminism

I'm not a feminist, but I support a woman's right to have an abortion. I'm not a feminist, but I believe in equal pay for equal work. I'm not a feminist, but I organized a campaign against sexual harassment at my school. And so it goes, the litany of statements in support of feminist issues, accompanied by the stark disclaimer. A major project of contemporary feminism is encouraging "I'm not…but" feminists to embrace the label whole-heartedly, while also recognizing that in many ways the word is less important than the actions or ethos.

Postfeminism

Postfeminism is the notion that the feminist movement has outlived its usefulness, because, after all, we have a few female Senators, it's illegal to discriminate against women in job hiring, there's a women's pro basketball league, and record numbers of women are attending college.

While such sentiments do point to feminism's far-reaching success, they also tend to re-personalize the political by assigning any continuing gender-related struggles to individual circumstances. And that, my friends, isn't good for anybody. The truth is, painting ours as a postfeminist world gets everyone in power off the hook; it pretends that everything is peachy and suggests that if, for you, it isn't, then the problem lies with you and your personal choices, not with any larger systems of, oh, let's say patriarchy or capitalism or racism or classism.

Despite the fact that more people than ever embrace feminist causes, the word itself still suffers from image problems. Because feminism suggests that everything isn't hunky-dory, it forces people to acknowledge the problems that plague us. But rather than positioning all women as helpless victims, as many antifeminists claim, feminism offers women a sense of agency, history, and solidarity. It provides a structural framework for making sense of thorny personal issues, and it offers a shared commitment to resolve these issues. Instructive bumper-sticker slogan: "I'll be post-feminist in the post-patriarchy."

I'm a Feminist And ...

In the end, it doesn't really matter which labels you choose or reject. What matters is your commitment to challenging the notion that a person's gender should, by law or by rote, be an obstacle to civil and personal liberties. It's important to have a sense of feminism's complex history, but it's also crucial to know—and help others understand—that feminism isn't something that happened to your mother or grandmother and is now over. It's living, breathing, and evolving.

> *"Today's iteration of feminism might gain wider credibility by recognizing and adopting core aspects of women of color's experiences."*

The Women's Movement Is Forgetting Women of Color

Amy Alexander

In the following viewpoint, Amy Alexander argues that the current feminist movement is "tone deaf" to the realities of life in the real world for ordinary women, particularly women of color. The organizers of marches and other actions are out of touch with the people they should be advocating for. Criticizing what she calls "hashtag feminism," Alexander calls for modern feminism to not only recognize but to adopt certain crucial aspects of the lived experience of women of color. Alexander is the author of four nonfiction books.

As you read, consider the following questions:

1. In what way is the women's movement out of touch with women of color according to Alexander?
2. What are some of the problems mentioned in this essay that plague women of color more than white women?
3. What could the movement learn from women of color?

"Today's Feminism: Too Much Marketing, Not Enough Reality," by Amy Alexander, National Public Radio Inc., February 21, 2017. Reprinted by permission.

I'm a black woman of a certain age, a divorced mom of two teenagers who has no choice but to focus daily on the challenges of keeping a home, my family and myself on track. I'm college educated, work in media communications, am precariously middle class—and I am tired of what I witness of today's feminism.

I'd hoped that the Women's March might help me update my perception of feminism, at least as it is commonly portrayed and disseminated of late.

I'd followed the back and forth in the alternative and mainstream press during its hurried, urgent formation, and chalked up reports about internal squabbles over the race and class makeup of the group's leadership to the same kind of growing pains that beset every activist group that I've ever followed or covered during my years in newsrooms. But now, a month after the Women's March masterfully pulled off a massive protest in D.C. that also inspired similar ones in major American and global cities, my nascent investigation of the March 8 "general strike" and "Day Without Women" raised only more concerns, and a few questions, all located in what I see as a big void in today's marketing-driven expression of "feminism."

At this moment, whether expressed by the second-wave, Gloria Steinem wing, or the third-wave corporatist Sheryl Sandberg arm, or the rowdy, genitalia-obsessed Lena Dunham arm, it seems that "feminism" in 2017 is more concerned with promoting superficial trappings of genuine equality than with doing the tough work required to address the hard, cold facts of gender and racial inequality.

For example, across all US occupations, women's median weekly earnings are $706 per week, compared with $860 for men, and the top 30 occupations for women cover a range of essential—but relatively low-paying—jobs such as elementary school teachers, administrative assistants, customer service representatives and retail sales, according to the most recent data available (2013) from the United States Bureau of Labor Statistics Women's Bureau. And, while black and Latina women together make up nearly

18 million of the total number of America's 67 million working women, they are disproportionately more likely to be heads of households, yet also more likely to receive less pay than white women and white men.

Moreover, in addition to stubborn disparities in the workforce and incomes, women of color see huge gaps between themselves and white men and women in health outcomes and other key life-expectancy indicators.

The Women's March, while apparently "led" by a diverse collection of black, white, Latina and Asian women from across age groups, is the latest entry in a recent bumper crop of "feminist movements," "collectives," "initiatives" that claim inclusivity and egalitarian principles, but which somehow always seem tone-deaf, at best, to the daily, on-the-ground realities of nonfamous black women and Latinas.

How, then, will working-class black women and Latinas respond to the idea of missing a day of work in a general strike as part of political resistance? It is a case of high-minded ideology that, while well-meaning, doesn't take into account the fact that some women can't miss even a single day of work without fear of being fired or docked a full day's pay. Consider that the "Day Without Immigrants," on Feb. 16—organized by disparate workers' and immigrant rights organizations in response to President Trump's proposal to build a wall between the US and Mexico, and to impose a strict immigration ban on seven Middle Eastern nations—resulted in private companies in several cities firing dozens of workers who participated in the boycott.

While the symbolism of the "Day Without Immigrants" is certainly valuable, for the immigrant and women workers who got fired for participating, and who now must find new jobs, you have to wonder if they now genuinely believe they received appropriate return on their investment. I have similar concerns about the upcoming "Day Without Women." As Jessa Crispin noted in a recent essay, "the pro-woman power elite peers deeply into

Marketing Not Feminism

Brands are often ready to adopt a feminist persona to appeal to women, who make up an powerful sector of the American consumer base. Yet, some marketers still treat women as a niche audience, creating gendered versions of everyday products.

Perhaps one of the longest-running marketing-to-women campaigns, tobacco companies have been advertising cigarettes to women for over 100 years. Nursing@USC's online Family Nurse Practitioner program created a timeline that shows how tobacco companies branded cigarettes as a symbol of feminist emancipation while highlighting false benefits of smoking, like weight loss and stress management. With slim, light and flavored cigarettes designed to appeal to women and girls with celebrity-sponsored ads, the tobacco industry overpowered public health officials' attempts to educate women and still sells cigarettes to 15 percent of American women today.

Perhaps the most obvious appropriation of feminism since the American Tobacco Company sponsored Amelia Earhart in the 1920s, Swiffer featured a model dressed like Rosie the Riveter to sell home cleaning products in 2013. The company quickly apologized for the ad, but not before critics took to Twitter over the controversy, citing sexism throughout advertisements for many cleaning companies that repeatedly feature women as the primary users of their products.

Marketing failures like Bic's Pens "For Her" show us that women are increasingly aware of the superficial ways that brands try to appeal to female consumers. In the ill-advised 2012 campaign, Bic launched a set of pens in feminine packaging that featured a "thin barrel for a woman's hand." Following a storm of criticism on Twitter, Amazon and an entire episode of *The Ellen Show*, Bic discontinued the line.

It's clear that the internet makes it possible for more women to be educated about the story behind marketing campaigns and the quality of products, but it also serves as a watchdog for companies that are seeking to capitalize off of women as a niche consumer base.

As long as women are watching with an analytical eye, brands will have to stay authentic through their manufacturing and advertising strategies.

"When Feminism Became a Marketing Technique," by Halah Flynn, *Girls' Globe*, April 24, 2017.

the savage inequalities of American life and asks, 'Where's my half of the profits?'"

Akin to the debate over white privilege, the debate over feminism is similarly stuck in a binary construct, largely defined in middle- or upper-middle-class white-lady contexts. Variations exist along generational lines: See the Lena Dunham crowd contrasted against the Steinem wing. But the marketing of modern feminism, and the oxygen-sucking place it holds in the public imagination, is largely occupied by white women.

The occasional invocation of Audre Lorde, Fannie Lou Hamer or Angela Davis by some leaders within these status quo or emerging white feminist camps in 2017 is notable—if also to me superficial and insufficient. (Yes, I know Davis is among a group of women who are advocating for a general strike.)

Today's purveyors of hashtag feminism exemplified by pink "pussy hats," safety pins and cheeky-ballsy slogans on T-shirts have forgotten that women of color have to learn how to navigate not only their own universes but also those of white women and men to literally be able to pay the rent and afford decent schools. We have to succeed in both spheres not only to achieve success, but to fundamentally cope. To ask us, then, to participate in a Lysistrata-like action makes me wonder if the gesture is designed more to give white ladies another opportunity for displaying unity, a kind of safari solidarity, than it is to provide women of color and working-class women tangible relief.

However out of fashion it is to say so in the wake of the 2016 presidential election, identity politics are inherently personal. Identity politics do, in fact, drive political outcomes, which in turn drive policy, economic and social developments.

I don't now and never have viewed the conventional version of feminism as a defining part of my identity; rather, based on what I have experienced and learned from the black women I've known my entire life, I have absorbed a degree of resilience, appreciation for common sense, and unflashy problem-solving that many women of color demonstrate. It is no accident that Black Lives

Matter was co-founded by Alicia Garza, Opal Tometi and Patrisse Cullors in the wake of the death of 18-year-old Michael Brown in Ferguson, Mo. Within the span of two years, BLM expanded into an effort to organize the energies and intellect of people of color and whites toward strategically resisting police brutality and other American institutions where systemic race and gender discrimination put us at risk. The energy and determination of BLM, its ability to spur dozens of protests nationwide since 2014, garnering condemnations from some police unions and elected politicians, seems to have inspired organizers of the Women's March without, apparently, deeply informing the group about the full range of potential negative consequences for participants.

Telling also is the group's tepid nod to intersectionality, the concept coined by Kimberlé Williams Crenshaw, a black legal scholar, which has informed the positions and actions of many emerging protest movements in recent years. Crenshaw's concept of intersectionality—the critical analysis of gender, ethnic and class aspects that drive inequality in populations and social structures—was earlier identified as "interlocking" factors by Chicana playwright Cherríe Moraga. This intellectual trait, the ability to recognize the multidimensional layers of inequality, are bedrocks of effective leadership across disciplines—although when demonstrated by women of color they are rarely characterized as such by the dominant society.

Today's iteration of feminism might gain wider credibility by recognizing and adopting core aspects of women of color's experiences: resilience, self-love and fundamental understanding that one's self-worth is not defined by the same markers of success that have defined white male status since the beginning of time in America.

> "In order to be considered a feminist,
> you only need to be on board with
> one idea: All humans, male and
> female, should have equal political,
> economic and social rights."

Despite Many Gains for Women, We Still Need Feminism

Casey Cavanagh

In the following viewpoint, Casey Cavanagh argues that, although women have achieved many gains, a feminist movement is still very much needed. However, women need to understand that the movement is ever evolving. Progress should not lead to total satisfaction and complacency. The author returns to the nuts and bolts of the feminist movement, and using less ideology and many facts compared to previous viewpoints, brings the debate back down to earth. She explains what feminism is at its most basic, and then gives very specific examples of why she believes we still need it. Cavanagh is a Boston-based freelance writer and editor.

"Why We Still Need Feminism," by Casey Cavanagh, Oath Inc., November 18, 2014. Reprinted by permission.

As you read, consider the following questions:

1. In what way are people misguided about what feminism really means, according to this author?
2. Does Cavanagh's description of feminism seem different from the movement the previous authors described?
3. Does the author make a strong case that we still need feminism?

Feminists are not angry lesbians who hate men. Feminists do not believe women are better than men, or that women deserve special privileges. They do not believe women are victims.

In order to be considered a feminist, you only need to be on board with one idea: All humans, male and female, should have equal political, economic and social rights.

Although more and more people are beginning to understand the true definition of feminism and openly identifying with it, there has always been a negative stigma attached to it. Part of this problem is the way our media sensationalizes things, trying to pass the most radical and extreme versions as the standard which, in this case, depicts a feminist as a man-hater who hates lipstick, crinkles her nose at stay-at-home moms, and unapologetically supports abortions on demand.

It's these false assumptions that cause anti-feminist campaigns, such as the recent "Women Against Feminism," which consists of people posting photos of themselves with statements such as: "I don't need feminism because I don't choose to ignore the fact that men have issues too" and "I don't need feminism because I already have equal rights." Reading through the majority of these posts quickly brings forth a glaringly obvious problem: how misguided too many people still are about what being a feminist actually means.

As Lena Dunham pointed out, "Feminism isn't a dirty word. It's not like we're a deranged group who think women should take over the planet, raise our young on our own and eliminate men from the picture."

Being a feminist has nothing to do with how you look, what you wear, who you date, or how often you have sex. Being a feminist doesn't mean you think women deserve special rights; it means you know we deserve equal ones.

While a primary purpose of feminism is to empower women, it does not mean feminists view all women as weak and oppressed. Feminists are not aiming to make women stronger; they already know they're strong. They just want society to see that too.

Empowering women does not mean belittling or punishing men. Men, too, suffer from gender role assumptions that place expectations upon them to live and act a certain way. Feminists believe each person should be viewed based on their individual strengths and capabilities as a human being, not the strengths and capabilities assumed of their gender. They believe every person should be treated equally—not because of gender, but in spite of it.

Why We Still Need Feminism

There are some people who believe that feminism is a thing of the past—that we don't need it anymore because the patriarchal system no longer exists. After all, we can vote, right? That's true. In fact, in all demographics, females vote more than men do. Yet, women still hold less than 20 percent of seats in Congress, even though they make up more than half the population. Some believe the patriarchal system doesn't exist because we have equal employment opportunities. But if this were really the case would there still be a 23 percent pay gap?

It is great so many women today feel like they have equal opportunities as men. If it wasn't for past feminist movements, who knows where we would be today. But we still need feminism, and will continue to need it, until every other woman in the world feels this way as well.

We still need feminism because when people get married it is assumed the woman will take the man's last name. Because when women are assaulted, they are often the ones who feel ashamed.

We still need feminism because we teach women how to prevent rape, instead of teaching people to not view women as objects. Because women are told that walking alone at night makes them "an easy target." Because, sometimes, a movie's rating (PG-13 versus R) depends on how much a female appears to be enjoying sex in a certain scene.

We still need feminism because our bodies are still being legislated, because McDonald's still asks us if we want a girl or boy toy, because we use terms like "bitch" and pussy" to imply weakness.

We need feminism because FGM (Female Genital Mutilation), the act of cutting off and restitching female genitals to prevent pleasurable sex—and can happen to girls as young as 5 months old—is still practiced in 29 countries. Because more than 120 countries don't have laws against marital rape, and still allow child brides—some as young as 6 years old.

We need feminism because infanticides, the act of killing children within a year of birth, has caused there to be millions fewer females than males in Middle Eastern countries, and because in Afghanistan women going to college can be considered justifiable grounds for disfiguring.

Being a feminist does not mean you think women can't speak for themselves, it means you realize that, even though some may be lucky enough to, there are still many who can't.

It Is Not a Gender Issue—It Is a Humanity Issue

It isn't about telling women what to do, it is giving them the ability and freedom to be able to choose to do whatever they want to do—whether that be a stay at home mom, electrical engineer, or business CEO. The purpose is to create a society of equal say, to provide people with the freedom of choice, rather than limited choices of assumption.

Feminists don't believe women should look or behave a certain way, it means they want women have to have the freedom to look and behave however they want—unapologetically. It is not about telling women what they need.

While reading through Women Against Feminism posts that say things such as, "I don't need it because I already feel equal" and "I don't want feminism because I don't need special treatment, and don't support sleeping around," I can't help but think it isn't about our personal wants and needs, though they are all relevant, but rather what we—as a society—needs.

If you are a feminist, you believe women should be treated the same as men, not because we're better, but because we're human.

As Joseph Gordon-Levitt so eloquently worded it, "I'm a believer that if everyone has a fair chance to be what they want to be and do what they want to do, it's better for everyone. It benefits society as a whole."

The idea that there are still people, let alone women, proudly declaring they don't need feminism is alarming and frightening—at best.

We need feminism because people are still blindly agreeing that women don't need to be paid for the same work as men, that they are okay with the indifference and injustices so ingrained in society that they have accepted it as a way of life. That they are not only looking the other way to these issues, but they are also entirely and genuinely convinced they are doing the world a favor by hushing feminist attempts.

Some people don't feel the need to voice their thoughts on the matter at all, and that's okay. But there is a big difference between being indifferent and being ignorant. And that difference is speaking out about an issue when your opinion is based on misguided information and false assumptions.

Why do we need feminism? For the same reason screenwriter John Whedon gave when asked why he writes such strong female characters, "Because you're still asking me that question."

> "The increasing commercialization
> of beauty, sex, and—at its core—
> the female body are ever-present
> challenges for feminists."

Feminism Must Address the Issue of Exploitation of Women's Bodies

Cayce D. Utley

In the following viewpoint, Cayce Utley argues that there is a pervasive problem with using women's bodies to sell both products and sex—both soft, marketing porn, and hard-core porn. She examines how feminists' attitudes about pornography have changed over the years, and how they vary among individuals and groups. This viewpoint challenges feminists to make the connections between the various means of exploitation of women and their bodies, and points out how pro-life feminists have led this effort. Utley is a policy analyst advocate for racial justice.

As you read, consider the following questions:

1. Why is pornography ultimately a feminist issue?
2. How do some modern feminists embrace pornography?
3. How does pornography increase instances of sex trafficking, according to the viewpoint?

In 1963, Gloria Steinem shocked America with her undercover exposé of the denigration women experienced working in Hugh Hefner's Playboy Club. Almost half a century later, Hefner parades his "bunnies" around on their own reality show while young girls across the country slap bunny stickers on the bumpers of their first cars. In fall 2011, NBC advertised its new serial drama, *The Playboy Club*, as a glamorous recreation of the club's early days: "It's the early 1960s, and at the center of Chicago lies the legendary and seductive Playboy Club, a living, breathing fantasy world filled with $1.50 cocktails, music, glitter, and of course, beautiful Bunnies." Pornography has become a staple of the mainstream and, as a result, has affected how two generations understand sex, violence, and human worth.

Over a decade ago, Cornell University professor Joan Jacobs Brumberg had a revelation in her classroom. During a talk on Victorian culture's dictates about women's bodies, her students began to open up about the pressures they face in modern society. The professor says, "These young women were bright enough to gain admission to an Ivy League university, and they enjoyed educational opportunities unknown to earlier generations. But they also felt a need to strictly police their bodies… Today, unlike in the Victorian era, commercial interests play directly into the body angst of young girls… Although elevated body angst is a great boost to corporate profits, it saps the creativity of girls and threatens their mental and physical health."

These conversations sparked Brumberg's book, *The Body Project: An Intimate History of American Girls*, in which she examines the historical shift in young women's attitudes about their bodies. She writes, "At the close of the twentieth century, the female body poses an enormous problem for American girls, and it does so because of the culture in which we live… [T]he current body problem is not just an external issue resulting from a lack of societal vigilance or adult support; it has also become an internal, psychological problem: Girls today make the body into an all-consuming project in ways young women of the past did not."

Brumberg identifies a serious problem for young women that feminists have been studying and discussing for decades. The increasing commercialization of beauty, sex, and—at its core—the female body are ever-present challenges for feminists. Naomi Wolf calls the marketing and glamorization of supposedly "flawless" standards of beauty in the media, etc., "beauty pornography." In her book, The Beauty Myth, she writes, "If women feel ugly, it is our fault, and we have no inalienable right to feel sexually beautiful. A woman must not admit it if she objects to beauty pornography because it strikes to the root of her sexuality by making her feel sexually unlovely. Male or female, we all need to feel beautiful… in the sense of welcome, desired, and treasured. Deprived of that, one objectifies oneself or the other for self-protection."

Young women affected by these expectations realize something is wrong but are often unable to articulate it. Talking to students, Wolf found that the concept of "beauty pornography" remained elusive to young women being influenced by it. After explaining the politics, symbolism, and cultural exclusion of the problem to a group of students, one woman told her, "I'll support you, though I have no idea what you're talking about. All I know is [these images] make me feel incredibly bad about myself." Wolf and Joan Jacobs Brumberg are not alone in their experiences working with young women who feel pressured by cultural norms of beauty and sexuality. Other feminists point out the connections between the commercialization of women for selling products (what Wolf calls "soft-core beauty pornography") and the commercialization of women for selling sexual experiences (what is widely recognized as "pornography"). Because these norms are so widely accepted, many women—including those who consider themselves feminists—are reluctant to confront the pervasive influence of porn culture. Today, not only are women expected to maintain trim, shapely physiques, they are sold the opportunity to do so through pole-dancing aerobics classes and Carmen Electra's Fit to Strip DVD.

British columnist Natasha Walter received a tremendous response to an article she wrote about pornographic magazines.

One young woman who wrote to her prompted Walter to explore the subject further in her book, *Living Dolls*. The 17-year-old wrote that she was "starting to think it was time to give up and sit in silence while my friends put on a porno… What you said gave me back the will not to give in… It's nice to see someone else saying it, makes me feel like less of a prude-type oddball."[5\]

Journalist Kira Cochrane writes of *Living Dolls*, "Walter takes on the notion that, for example, stripping and pole-dancing are empowering, liberating choices; instead she suggests, it has become increasingly difficult for young women to opt out of this culture." Walter says about the research she conducted for her book, "I was surprised by the attitudes of the girls I interviewed who seemed to feel that they would be mocked if they protested within their peer groups. You know, when I was at university [in the '80s], it was OK to be annoyed about sexism… [Y]ou could still say, 'I really don't want Page 3 in the common room,' or, 'I really hate the idea of porn.'"

Anti-pornography activist and Wheelock College professor Gail Dines says, "A key sign that pornography is now deeply embedded in our culture is the way it has become synonymous with sex to such a point that to criticize pornography is to get slapped with the label 'anti-sex'… Porn sex is a sex that is debased, dehumanized, formulaic, and generic, a sex based not on individual fantasy, play or intimacy, but one that is the result of an industrial product created by men who get excited not by bodily contact but by profits." In her book, *Pornified*, Pamela Paul writes, "Habitual male consumers of mainstream pornography—that is, nonviolent but nonetheless objectifying images—appear to be at greater risk of becoming sexually callous toward female sexuality and concerns."

An early tenet of the feminist movement was an opposition to the objectification of women in the media in general and in pornography in particular. Pro-life feminists continue that legacy today, emphasizing the connections between violence against women and pornography. Some pro-choice feminists share that conviction, even while others in their movement embrace porn culture as an opportunity for women to explore their own sexuality. This division within the feminist movement became heated in the late 1970s during the "pornography wars," in which "two distinct and oppositional factions developed. On the one hand, there were the anti-porn feminists and on the other, there were the women who felt that if feminism was about freedom, then women should be free to look at or appear in pornography."

Ariel Levy, author of *Female Chauvinist Pigs: Women and the Rise of Raunch Culture* and writer for The New Yorker magazine, adds that the pro-choice feminist movement made an early uneasy alliance with Playboy founder Hugh Hefner: "Roe and the legalization of the birth control pill—both of which were crucial to feminists—were both helped by funding from Hefner.... But a shared distaste for conventional family arrangements and repressive laws was the extent of Hefner's ideological compatibility with the women's liberation movement." Levy says of the mismatch, "[Hefner's statements about his bunnies] made feminists want to throw up. They were specifically fighting to be seen as real people, not sudsy bunnies. They wanted to show the world that women were 'difficult' and 'sophisticated,' not to mention formidable."

In her essay "Pornography and the Sexual Revolution," FFL activist Judy Shea writes, "It is no accident that the greatest apologist for pornography in our culture, Hugh Hefner, is also enthusiastic about abortion on demand.... The reality of the possibility of pregnancy and childbirth interferes with the Hefner dream of multiple partners and everlasting orgies. The Hefner playboy is incapable of relating to a mature woman who ovulates, menstruates, conceives, and lactates. In fact, he's quite puritanical about the messy, dirty processes of human reproduction. He likes his bunnies 'clean' and sterile."

Unapologetic anti-porn feminists pulled away from the mainstream and formed a prominent "splinter group of activists, including [Susan] Brownmiller, Gloria Steinem, Shere Hite, Robin Morgan, the poet Adrienne Rich, and the writers Grace Paley and Audre Lorde." Brownmiller and others founded the New York

FEMINISM AS FASHION TREND

Today everyone, it seems, is a feminist. Practically every female pop icon, actress, and model has proclaimed herself to be a feminist.

Once a movement dedicated to improving the lives of women of all shapes, colors, and sizes, feminism has gone commercial—and upmarket. Indeed, feminism today is more a fashion statement than a political cause pursuing equality for women. Just ask Dior. For its Spring 2017 collection, Dior joined the feminist movement with a white tee that reads "We Should All Be Feminists".

The commercialization of feminism, in my opinion, is detrimental to the entire movement. Feminism has abandoned its core values and transformed into something that can be defined and customized differently by each woman, depending on her purpose. When women define what feminism means to them, they tend to forget it's about equality for all women. They are focused on themselves. It has become like buying a luxury T-shirt.

All the hype and celebrity endorsements surrounding universal feminism do not represent the critical issues women face every day. The media has shaped mainstream feminism, undermining the fundamental purpose of feminism and ignoring the realities of working women, poor women, rural women, whose voices are not heard, and who live outside the cultured metropolitan areas where mainstream feminists live. Sadly, the voice of feminism has become a link on social media, an article in *Huffington Post*, a brand or celebrity trying to sell a product or support a movement. Feminism has become not so much anymore about seeking equality, but more about self-empowerment and personal gain.

"Feminism Has Become the Superficial Fashion Trend of the Decade," by Sabrina Aguirre, *Peacock Plume*, May 7, 2017.

chapter of Women Against Pornography and began tackling the problem right outside their office on 42nd Street.

Levy writes, "The area was a swamp of peep shows, porn shops, and prostitution—ground zero for the objectification of women—and the feminists set up camp right in the middle of it…. Women

Against Pornography's trademark was offering guided tours of the neighborhood intended to elucidate the degradation of sex workers. They would bring visiting Benedictine nuns to a strip club to observe the patrons and dancers, or they'd take a curious band of housewives inside a porn shop so they could investigate what it was their husbands were looking at in the garage."

Feminists like these working against pornography in the late '70s and early '80s sought to address the degradation and objectification of women at every level of society. They also saw their foe for what it was: an industry made wealthy by the consistent and pervasive dehumanization of women.

According to feminist activist, professor, and author Robert Jensen, pornography is a booming industry: "The fact that more than ten billion dollars a year is spent on pornography makes it very clear that pornography does not express a deviant sexuality. It, in fact, expresses a very conventional sexuality, and that means the road takes us not just to the valley in California where this material is produced. It takes us into our own lives and into our own bedroom." A recent *Newsweek* study led by Melissa Farley, the director of Prostitution Research and Education, looked at the growing demand for prostitution. The team of researchers found that "buying sex is so pervasive that Farley's team had a shockingly difficult time locating men who really don't do it. The use of pornography, phone sex, lap dances, and other services has become so widespread that the researchers were forced to loosen their definition in order to assemble a 100-person control group."

Farley said, "We had big, big trouble finding nonusers. We finally had to settle on a definition of non-sex-buyers as men who have not been to a strip club more than two times in the past year, have not purchased a lap dance, have not used pornography more than one time in the last month, and have not purchased phone sex or the services of a sex worker, escort, erotic masseuse, or prostitute." Buying porn and patronizing businesses that profit from the sexual exploitation of women has become culturally expected of men. Robert Jensen frankly confronts men about the objectification of women in pornography in his essay, "A Cruel Edge: The Painful Truth About Today's Pornography—and What Men Can Do About It." He writes, "Men spend $10 billion on pornography a year. 11,000 new pornographic films are made every year. And in those films, women are not people. In pornography, women are three holes and two hands."

Jensen adds, "All of these acts are, at their base, about male domination and female submission. Men's ability to do whatever they want to do to women and women accepting it, and even further in pornography, not only women accepting it, but women seeing it as part of their nature." It is this dehumanization and emphasis on male power that makes pornography dangerous. One of the most pressing concerns for feminists today is the ever-increasing levels of violence in popular pornography. In the documentary *The Price of Pleasure*, Dr. Ana Bridges, psychology professor at the University of Arkansas says, "Defenders of pornography often state that critics hold up the worst-case examples, most degrading, most violent pornography and talk about why this is harmful. But in fact, pornography is very diverse." In a study on violence and aggression in pornography, Dr. Bridges and her research team examined 304 scenes from the most popular porn videos released in 2005. The team found that 89.8 percent of the scenes contained verbal or physical aggression. Ninety-four percent of the aggressive acts in those scenes were targeted at women.

Anti-porn activist Robin Morgan once said, "Pornography is the theory, rape is the practice." Neil Malamuth, a psychologist well-known for his studies of the aftereffects of pornography, concluded in a literature review, "Experimental research shows that exposure to nonviolent or violent pornography results in increases in both attitudes supporting sexual aggression and in actual aggression." He adds from his own study, "When we considered men who were previously determined to be at high risk for sexual aggression.... we found that those who are additionally very frequent users of pornography were much more likely to have engaged in sexual aggression than their counterparts who consume pornography less frequently." Naomi Wolf argues that pornography not only desensitizes men and women to violence, it normalizes violence: "Cultural representation of glamorized degradation has created a situation among the young in which boys rape and girls get raped as a normal course of events."

Besides pornography's profitable homage to violence against women, the industry itself thrives upon the victimization of women. Porn buyers are led to believe that the women they see in the magazines want to be there. Buyers are conditioned to think that the transaction is consensual and the materials they are viewing are harmless. Yet this "legitimacy" of pornography often provides a legal front for trafficking operations. Linda Smith, founder and president of Shared Hope International and former member of Congress, says that traffickers use "spotters" to lure young women into the commercial sex industry and from there into prostitution. Shared Hope International, working with the American Center for Law and Justice, has released a model legislative framework for targeting pornographers as facilitators and perpetrators of sex trafficking.

Porn's first big "star," Linda Lovelace, wrote in her book *Ordeal* about her start in porn, orchestrated by an abusive and controlling husband who acted as manager and manipulator. Other women report having been coerced, abused, and manipulated into performing in pornographic films. According to Laura Lederer, former Senior Advisor on Human Trafficking at the US State Department, porn also increases the demand for sex trafficking because it sends the messages that it's "normal" for men to exploit women and girls for their own pleasure, and it's "glamorous" for women to be used and abused in this way. Lederer says, "Pornography is a brilliant social marketing campaign for sexual exploitation."

Because pornography has been normalized in American culture—even celebrated as a liberating force by both women and men—combating it is a tremendous challenge for pro-life feminists and pro-choice anti-porn feminists. For many years, feminist groups have worked independently to put pressure on the porn industry, approaching the problem both as academics and activists. But these isolated efforts could be strengthened. Laura Lederer responds, "If our challenge at the end of the 20th century was to recognize that sexual exploitation is a growing phenomenon... our challenge in the 21st century is to link up all of our various efforts. We must do it. We have to make the connections between the various forms of sexual exploitation, sex trafficking and sex slavery." Pro-life feminists make those connections and, in doing so, become the voice of those threatened and exploited by pornography.

> "*Far from the idea that women working outside the home for pay is a matter of individual preference, most women work because they must.*"

The Family Values Agenda Is an Attack on Working-Class Families

Jen Roesch

In the following excerpted viewpoint Jen Roesch addresses the issues facing feminists today from the perspective of class. Roesch examines the backlash to the feminist movement that has occurred in the past few decades—particularly from the right wing family values movement. The author argues that much of the "family values" resistance to feminism is not merely an attack on women and the feminist movement, but an attack on working-class Americans (both male and female). Roesch is a New York-based socialist and activist.

"Turning Back the Clock? Women, Work and Family Today," by Jen Roesch, *International Socialist Review*, November-December 2004. Reprinted by permission.

As you read, consider the following questions:

1. According to Roesch's analysis, how does the family values agenda actually harm women and, perhaps more surprisingly, children?
2. How have the media and family values advocates misrepresented women's reasons for working outside the home according to the viewpoint?
3. After reading several viewpoints that at least touch on this issue, why do you think feminism is so intertwined with issues of class?

Thirty-five years ago, the women's liberation movement raised the hopes and expectations of a generation of women. This movement challenged the prevailing notion that women were supposed to spend their entire lives engaged in housework and raising children. It demanded equal pay for women in the workplace, publicly funded child care, and the legalization of abortion.

It challenged sexist stereotypes of women and the ideal of the traditional nuclear family, which often tied women to abusive or oppressive relationships. While the Ozzie and Harriet myth of the nuclear family—with a male breadwinner and stay-at-home mother—never really existed for many working-class Americans, the women's liberation movement altered people's ideas about the role of women in society on a mass scale.

Today, both the ideological and the material gains of the women's movement have come under a sustained attack. This backlash has its roots in the assault on working-class people over the last three decades. The intent of this class attack has been two-fold: to roll back the social gains of the late 1960s and early 1970s and to transfer wealth upward. This has meant a gutting of working-class living standards at the same time as the social safety net has been systematically shredded.

The backlash against the gains of the women's movement has mirrored these two trends. On an ideological level, a right-wing "family values" agenda has reversed the most basic assumptions of the women's movement about the nuclear family and women's role within it. On an economic level, working-class women and children have been subjected to a devastating series of attacks, while more and more responsibility for children's welfare has been placed on individual families.

[...]

There is an urgent need to discuss the real state of women and their families today. But the traditional women's organizations are either unwilling or unable to take up the challenge. For millions, the promises of the women's liberation movement have failed to materialize, and the language and politics of feminism have been unable to explain the gap. The aim of this article is to show how the ideological backlash against the gains of the women's movement has accompanied a material assault on women and children; to examine the reality of women and the family today; to offer an explanation of why the women's movement failed to deliver for the majority of women; and to argue what it would take to win genuine liberation today.

Restoring the Family

The main ideological aim of the backlash has been to reassert the centrality of the traditional nuclear family. This has meant undermining many of the most basic ideas of the women's movement: that women should be able to freely leave unhappy marriages; that women can combine work and family; that a woman's right to control her own body is fundamental to equality.

[...]

While conservatives often couch their proposals in soft and "compassionate" language, the actual policies they advocate are reactionary. They aim to repeal no-fault divorce laws, re-stigmatize single motherhood, and take away women's right to control their own bodies. Because conservatives consider the restoration of the traditional nuclear family as the primary goal, they often oppose measures that would actually improve families' lives, such as child care funding or paid maternity leave. As a member of the conservative Family Research Council put it: "Providing child care is a distraction from our main goal of helping married women stay home to raise their kids. If you make it easier for mothers to have careers, you also reward divorce and illegitimacy."[1]

Opt-Out Revolution?

While the Christian Right has long championed the return of the traditional family, today the media is busy trying to sell the idea of a "post-feminist" revolution in women's attitudes toward work and family. The pundits of post-feminism argue that women have achieved equality and are now suffering from an excess of liberation. They would like us to believe that the daughters of the Gloria Steinem generation are abandoning the workplace to dedicate themselves to the more fulfilling realm of home and family.

In recent years, there has been a proliferation of articles, news stories, and books heralding this supposed phenomenon. An article that ran in the *New York Times Magazine* in October 2003 is typical. Titled "The Opt-Out Revolution," the story ran on the front cover of the magazine with the provocative statement: "Why don't women run the world? Maybe it's because they don't want to."[2]

In the article, Lisa Belkin, the *Times*' life-work correspondent, examines a small group of Yale and Princeton graduates who have chosen to leave behind the corporate world to stay home with their children. From this small and unrepresentative sampling, she concludes that there is a significant trend of women choosing to become stay-at-home mothers. She paints this not as a return to traditional values but as the new wave in feminism: "This is not the failure of a revolution, but the start of a new one."[3]

Yet many of the sentiments expressed in the article are a throwback to the 1950s. For example, a large proportion of her story is devoted to the idea that women are biologically conditioned to play a nurturing and child-rearing role. She claims that much of the conversation among women today is "not about how the workplace is unfair to women, but about how the relationship between work and life is different for women than for men." She quotes one mother saying, "I think some of us are swinging to a place where we enjoy, and can admit we enjoy, the stereotypical role of female/mother/caregiver. I think we were born with those feelings."[4]

In addition, this group of privileged women shuns any connection to an actual movement for women's equality. In the words of one woman: "I don't want to take on the mantle of all womanhood and fight a fight for some sister who isn't really my sister because I don't even know her."[5]

Just a few months after the Belkin story, *Time* magazine ran a similar article on its cover called "The Case for Staying Home." Reading through the article, one discovers a story of long work hours necessary to make ends meet, inflexible workplace policies, and enormous societal pressure on mothers. However, the conclusion the editors chose to run on the front page was: "Caught between the pressures of the workplace and the demands of being a mom, more women are sticking with the kids."[6] In the climate of post-feminist family values, a story that might have been an opportunity to expose the difficult demands of the workplace becomes another argument for women returning home.

Susan J. Douglas and Meredith W. Michaels, the authors of the book *The Mommy Myth*, refer to "the new momism." They describe how the media has created an unattainable ideal of the mother who can "do it all"—while removing the social supports (welfare, child care funding, preschool education, etc.) that working mothers so desperately need. This has left women to conclude that, if they are unable to successfully manage the multiple demands of paid work, housework, and child care, it is their own personal failure. Women who work are fed heavy doses of guilt as news stories about bad day care, latchkey kids, and the dangers of "detached parenting" fill the airwaves.

The authors show how the ideas of women's liberation have been turned on their head by this campaign:

The mythology of the new momism now insinuates that, when all is said and done, the enlightened mother chooses to stay home with the kids. Back in the 1950s, mothers stayed home because they had no choice, so the thinking goes. Today, having been to the office, having tried a career, women supposedly have seen the inside of the male working world and found it to be the inferior choice to staying home, especially when their kids' future is at stake. It's not that mothers can't hack it (1950s thinking). It's that progressive mothers refuse to hack it. Inexperienced women thought they knew what they wanted, but they got experience and learned they were wrong. Now mothers have seen the error of their ways, and supposedly seen that the June Cleaver model, if taken as a choice, as opposed to a requirement, is the truly modern, fulfilling, forward-thinking version of motherhood.[7]

The intent of all of this is to convince us that the institutional barriers that women faced in the past have been broken down (or at least mitigated) and replaced by a set of individual choices that they may pursue. As one woman put it, "Women today, if we think about feminism at all, we see it as a battle fought for 'the choice.' For us, the freedom to choose work if we want to work is the feminist strain in our lives." The value of this notion to employers and politicians cannot be underestimated. It allows them to reframe the question of women's equality as one of personal achievement, rather than institutional change.

The main problem with the theory of women's recent return to the home is that it's simply not true. There is no sign of a mass exodus of women from the paid workforce. In fact women, including mothers, are doing the opposite; they are working longer and harder than ever before. In 2003, 78 percent of women with school-aged children, 59 percent of women with children under the age of five and 54 percent of women with infants worked for pay.[8]

Clearly, women are not heading home—and for a very simple reason. Far from the idea that women working outside the home for pay is a matter of individual preference, most women work because they must. In an era of increasing job insecurity and economic precariousness, 30 percent of working women make all or almost all of their family's income, and 60 percent earn half or more of their family's income.[9] Women's wages are not pocket change or disposable earnings that could be done without if only families would eat at home as some of the back-to-home crusaders argue. Women's wages have become increasingly crucial to families' ability to stay afloat.

In fact, the common problem with both the right-wing family values advocates and the pundits of the post-feminist revolution is that neither speaks to the actual reality of the majority of real women and children's lives. The family values crusaders may long for a return to the traditional family, but that family, to the extent that it ever existed, no longer does. Only 9 percent of people today live in the traditional nuclear family of two married parents with a wage-earning father and full-time mother.[10] The trend is toward a greater diversity of families. Today, families may be headed by a gay couple, a single mother, an unmarried couple, or a combination of biological and stepparents. Despite the media-induced anxiety about unwed mothers, divorce, and gay marriage, 90 percent of people, when polled, say society should value "all types of families."[11]

[…]

Endnotes

1. Stephanie Coontz, *The Way We Really Are: Coming to Terms With America's Changing Families* (New York: Perseus Books, 1997), 72.

2. Lisa Belkin, "Opt-Out Revolution," *New York Times Magazine*, October 26, 2003.

3. Ibid.

4. Ibid.

5. Ibid.

6. Claudia Walls, "The Case for Staying Home," *Time*, March 22, 2004.

7. Susan Douglas and Meredith Michaels, *The Mommy Myth: The Idealization of Motherhood and How It Has Undermined Women* (New York: Simon and Shuster, 2004), 23.

8. "Employment Characteristics of Families, Tables 4, 5 and 6," 2002—2003, US Department of Labor, Bureau of Labor Statistics, available online at: http://www.bls. gov/news.release/ famee.toc.htm.

9. "Ask A Working Woman Survey Report," 2004, AFL-CIO, available online at http:// www.aflcio.org/issuespolitics/women/_report/upload/aawwreport.pdf.

10. Cited in Sharon Smith, "Abortion Is Every Woman's Right," *Socialist Worker*, April 23, 2004.

11. Cited in Coontz, 94.

Periodical and Internet Sources Bibliography

The following articles have been selected to supplement the diverse views presented in this chapter.

Karen Grigsby Bates, Race and Feminism: Women's March Recalls the Touchy History. NPR.com, January 21, 2017. https://www.npr.org/sections/codeswitch/2017/01/21/510859909/race-and-feminism-womens-march-recalls-the-touchy-history

Susan Chira, "Feminism Lost. Now What?" *The New York Times*, December 30, 2016.https://www.nytimes.com/2016/12/30/opinion/sunday/feminism-lost-now-what.html

Carly Fiorina, "Redefining Feminism: The State of Women in America." *Medium*, June 24, 2015. https://medium.com/@CarlyFiorina/redefining-feminism-19d25d8d8dfc

Rachel Hirsch. "Can You Be Feminist and Pro-life? The Question Misses the Point." *ABC* (Australian Broadcasting Corporation), January 26, 2017. http://www.abc.net.au/news/2017-01-27/feminist-and-pro-life-question-misses-the-point/8214730

Tanja Jacobi and Dylan Schweers, "How Men Continue to Interrupt Even the Most Powerful Women." *Aeon*, May 26, 2017. https://aeon.co/ideas/how-men-continue-to-interrupt-even-the-most-powerful-women

Abigail Rine, "The Pros and Cons of Abandoning the Word Feminist." *The Atlantic*, May 2, 2017. https://www.theatlantic.com/sexes/archive/2013/05/the-pros-and-cons-of-abandoning-the-word-feminist/275511/

Sarah Smarsh, "Working-Class Women Are Too Busy for Gender Theory—but They're Still Feminists." *The Guardian*, June 25, 2017.https://www.theguardian.com/world/2017/jun/25/feminism-working-class-women-gender-theory-dolly-parton

Veena Venugopal, "Feminists Have Killed Feminism." *Blink*, March 10, 2017. http://www.thehindubusinessline.com/blink/talk/feminists-have-killed-feminism/article9577862.ece

Lane Windham, "From Pink Collars to Pink Hats: Working-class Feminism and the Resistance." *American Prospect*, March 29, 2017. http://prospect.org/article/pink-collars-pink-hats-working-class-feminism-and-resistance

OPPOSING
VIEWPOINTS®
SERIES

Why Are There So Few Women Leaders?

Chapter Preface

In this chapter, we shift from discussions of the ideologies and goals of feminism, to zero in on one of feminism's most glaring failures: the astonishing dearth of women in leadership positions. Women have made significant gains in recent years. More American women than men are college graduates; more women than men are enrolled in medical school; and women are, as of 2017, registering to run for political office in record numbers. However, women still struggle to advance as high in their careers as their male counterparts. The problem is particularly notable in technology fields, where women are often belittled, ignored, or harassed.

The pay gap between men and women is also a chronic problem for women who are trying to succeed in the business world. Even when the letter of the law is met regarding equal pay, women still make less money on average than men. This is partly due to the difficulties women have in getting better jobs and partly due to them being undervalued by their employers, resulting in lower compensation. Women are also less likely to be strong negotiators, and are more likely to take off time for child care or family emergencies, resulting in lower pay over the course of a career. These factors make it difficult to tease out the fundamental reasons for the pay gap and find adequate solutions.

The following viewpoints include a variety of positions on these issues. Experts here analyze the reasons women are less likely to succeed in the technology industry, make suggestions for how women in tech can improve the odds of success, offer a framework leaders can use to reduce gender bias in their organizations, and question the existence of the pay gap. The last piece turns from business to politics, analyzing the complex and fraught gender issues that surfaced in the 2016 US presidential election.

> *"At the end of the day, having a diverse workforce isn't just about a company feeling good about itself. McKinsey research indicates that gender-diverse companies outperform by 15%."*

The Tech Industry Benefits When Women Succeed There

Elizabeth Grace Becker

In the following viewpoint, Elizabeth Grace Becker argues that women face difficulties in the tech industry, from not having the right education to experiencing more harassment than women in other fields. Women struggle for parity in leadership roles in almost all businesses but they are especially under-represented in technology fields. The author gives advice for what women can do to mitigate each of these problems. She closes with a statement about why having a more diverse workforce is good for the industry. Becker is a writer who specializes in tech and workplace issues.

"Overcoming the challenges of being a woman in Tech," by Elizabeth Grace Becker, PROTECH, www.protechitjobs.com, March 27, 2017. Reprinted by permission. This was original published via PROTECH (www.protechitjobs.com) and used with permission from UXDesign.cc.

As you read, consider the following questions:

1. Why according to Becker, is it often better to train experts in other fields in tech skills, rather than the other way around?
2. What solution does the author suggest regarding the catch-22 women face over confidence?
3. How can being a woman in tech be an advantage according to the viewpoint?

With men comprising a high percentage of those in the tech space, it can be difficult as a woman trying to compete. Even tech giants like Google, Microsoft and Twitter have extremely low numbers of women in their tech roles. In 2015, women in tech roles at these companies were only 16.6 percent at Microsoft, 10 percent at Twitter and 17 percent at Google. When you look at the numbers in executive leadership roles (not just in tech), only 23 percent of Microsoft's leadership roles are filled by women, 21 percent at Twitter and 21 percent at Google.

Previously, I wrote about the "Highs and Lows of Women in Tech" to highlight some of the challenges women face in the industry. With thousands of shares, comments and likes, it was clear that it hit a chord in the tech space by highlighting the fact that there is still a lot of work to be done in the industry. As a follow-up to that piece, this covers the major challenges that women face in tech and avenues and advice from experts to address and potentially overcome those challenges.

Not Having the Right Education

With less than half of computer science students being women, many women that might have an interest in tech may not have the right education that employers are looking for. However, just because you didn't gain an education specifically in tech, doesn't mean it's too late to jump into the tech space. In fact, many companies have found that it's often easier to train a specialist to code than it is to train a programmer on a specific industry. Healthcare software companies actually hire doctors and train them in technology in order to design and build their EMR system. Who better to help design a health record system used by doctors than doctors themselves?

Stephanie Sylvestre, Chief Programs Officer/Chief Information Officer at The Children's Trust of Miami-Dade County, started her education in International Relations, but found she was able to use that knowledge to enter the tech space. "Back in the late 1990s when I got started, there was flexibility in knowledge of technology so I decided to give it a try," she said. "I found two things—one it's a high paying industry and two, I could transfer my education in international relations to analysis of computer systems. I was able to parlay that into a highly successful IT career. In 1995, I entered the IT vector without any experience, over 20 years later, I am CIO of a $100 million company because I kept learning and was okay with asking for help. Of course, being a great team player and having humility went a long way."

Deborah Vazquez, CEO of IT Staffing Firm PROTECH, believes that it's important in any career to have a plan and to leverage your skills to attain that goal. "I entered the tech field begging my way into a programming role after working as an assistant in an accounting department of a theatrical organization. I had purposely looked for a job where I could use the accounting skills I had gained, but where the opportunity existed to transition into a tech role."

There are also boot-camps and training programs like IronHack for both men and women that have realized a passion for tech after college. Programs like these allows students to use their current skills to transition into a tech focused role. There are also free ways to learn computer science.

The Confidence Gap

Unfortunately, women often are not confident or underestimate their skills. Reports show that female computer science concentrators with eight years of programming experience are as confident in their skills as their male peers with zero to one year of programming experience.

Some have a hard time believing in a confidence gap and that this is a simple case of men overestimating their skills and less about women lacking in confidence. Interestingly, it is a combination of both. In several studies, when men and women are given the same skills test and asked to self-assess, women give themselves an average score lower than their actual score and men give themselves an average score higher than their actual score. Both men and women score very similarly in a variety of skills tests (so there is little discernible differences between level of skill between sexes). In the programming example, this was an actual study done by Harvard that found men started their self-assessment (from 0–5) at about 3.3/5 with 0–6 months of experience. Women started much lower (2.6/5) and only self-assessed as a 3.3/5 after 8 years of experience. Men with that same experience self-assess at 4.3/5 after 8 years. Since it is unlikely that men will start lowering their own assessments and confidence, it is up to women to bridge the confidence gap.

In the recruiting space, I have seen this first hand, and often have to push female candidate to be more confident when talking about their abilities when preparing them for an interview. On the other hand, I have had male candidates with 6 months' experience tell me they were as strong as other candidates with 3+ years' experience. Confidence plays a big part in the tech space, and the unfortunate reality is that the male candidate with the 6 months' experience and confident attitude will land the job over another candidate, male or female, with several years of experience but lacking in confidence.

"Some observers say children change our priorities, and there is some truth in this claim. Maternal instincts do contribute to a complicated emotional tug between home and work lives, a tug that, at least for now, isn't as fierce for most men. Other commentators point to cultural and institutional barriers to female success. There's truth in that, too. But these explanations for a continued failure to break the glass ceiling are missing something more basic: women's acute lack of confidence," say Katty Kay and Claire Shipman on an inspiring article about the confidence gap for the *Atlantic*. Turns out, women hold themselves back in the workplace, often believing they aren't good enough, when chances are, they are as competent as their male peers. In fact, companies have tried to figure out why they have a lack of women in key leadership. A famous study by HP came to the startling conclusion that women were not applying for a promotion unless they met 100% of the requirements while men will happily apply if they only meet 60% of the requirements.

Women are holding themselves back in the confidence department. Katty Kay and Claire Shipman add, "We were curious to find out whether male managers were aware of a confidence gap between male and female employees. And indeed, when we raised the notion with a number of male executives who supervised women, they expressed enormous frustration. They said they believed that a lack of confidence was fundamentally holding back women at their companies, but they had shied away from saying anything, because they were terrified of sounding sexist."

Then of course there is the flip side. Women that are confident are told they are too aggressive, with 84% of women in tech reporting they have been told this, often more than once. 47% also have been asked to do lower-level tasks that male colleagues are not asked to do (e.g., note-taking, ordering food, etc.). With a very well-established confidence gap between the sexes, it is very possible that women that are simply confident come across negatively when compared to other woman, who may not have the same confidence traits.

"Confidence with a big 'C' is a myth," said Lerner, who founded WomenWorking.com, a career website for women. "We hold ourselves back from valuable opportunities if we wait for everything to line up and to have all our skills in place. [We] have to redefine confidence and understand that courage is the main ingredient for success for achieving their goals."

How can a woman in tech find the courage they need to succeed and excel in a career where their perception of their own skills is often most important?

Jill Flynn, partner at leadership consulting firm Flynn Heath Holt, recommends women stand up for themselves and their ideas, especially in meetings. "Meetings are so important because they're the corporate stage," Flynn said. Rather than observe, contribute to the meeting and do not be afraid of your idea being rejected. Confidence and courage are muscles that need to be flexed in order to grow, sharing an idea in a meeting might be scary the first time, but each time you speak up you will grow your confidence.

Women in tech also need to train themselves to use more direct language. Instead of using passive language like "what do you think about doing it like this?" women should instead use active language like "I suggest we should do it like this." Along with that, Flynn says we need to stop apologizing in the workplace.

Team sports also appear to play a big role in developing confidence for pre-teens, however, this is also the time when many girls tend to drop out of competitive programs. Confidence also stems from not being afraid of mistakes or failure—both of which are encouraged by competitive sports. As an adult, even if you missed out on being on the baseball team, there are still ways to build confidence including joining an adult sports league or competitive exercise programs. Exercise on a whole is a great confidence boost and adding in an element of competition can help boost your confidence in the workplace.

Finding a Support System

It's also important for women in tech to find a mentor, whether that is a relative or someone in the tech industry you admire. For Patti Barney, Vice President of Information Technology at Broward College, it was her grandfather that motivated her into the tech space. "My grandfather was an adjunct instructor in the technology field," she said. "He projected high demand and high wages for female careers in technology (back in the early 1980s—great insight!) I also saw it as an opportunity to learn many new things, innovation stems from ideas and creativity which was one of my strengths plus I preferred a challenge over "routine" every day of the week."

What makes someone a good mentor for you? The best mentor would be someone whose career you admire and are looking to mirror that you share a common connection with.

"The best mentors are often women that you establish a relationship with, that you find a connection with. And then it develops—and it takes on its own natural progression. And some of the best mentors you might never have the conversation about whether or not you're a mentor or a mentee. But you know it—and they play that role for you, and they're happy to do so. So, it isn't helpful for some women, in that, they really want to know specifically, tactically, 'How do I do this?' So the best advice that senior executive women have shared with me to pass along is that, you find a connection with these women. You put yourself out there, and get to know them—and, if they reciprocate with equal interest, then you keep going. And you build the relationship like you would any other relationship," says Wendy Cukier, Vice President Research and Innovation, and Founder & Director, Diversity Institute, Ryerson University.

For example, if you are looking to be a director of software engineering one day, find someone in this type of role through networking or company events and invite them to something informal, such a coffee or lunch. She also warns that asking someone to be your mentor is not the best approach. "On the subject of asking for a mentor itself, I have heard a consistent response from peers and influential women everywhere; they don't like to be asked. In fact, the general rule of thumb for finding a mentor seems to be that if you have to ask, it's probably not right."

Finding a mentor is similar to finding a significant other—best practices would advise against asking them to be your boyfriend or girlfriend on the first date. Instead, you work on building a relationship and getting to know each other—the key difference being you may never officially declare yourselves a mentor-mentee relationship—you're just two people at different career levels that enjoy learning from each other. Good mentorship relationships are not one-sided, your mentor is likely learning from you as well, perhaps to better understand those they manage in their team.

Vazquez believes that success as a woman in tech is less about gender and more about education, self-confidence and hard work. "My advice to young women is to seek out a mentor that understands your goals, appreciates your talents and is willing to help you succeed. This combined with a good attitude and tenacity has been the right formula for me. After many years in the software industry and a lot of domestic and overseas travel which was wearing on me, I pursued my entrepreneurial passion and founded PROTECH. This allowed me to once again do something that maximized technical and business skills in the software business to create unique value for our clients. I'm proud of the reputation and quality brand my team and I have built over the years. And much of what we do involves career coaching, which we enjoy very much."

Workplace Harassment

Along with being a minority in the workplace, many women report both harassment from their male counterparts and superiors. Shockingly, 60% of women in tech reported unwanted sexual advances with 65% of those advances being from a superior. For those that did report sexual assault, 60% were dissatisfied with the outcome. As a woman who has reported sexual assault to HR only to be told I should be "flattered" to be receiving attention, there is no easy solution for women when it comes to workplace sexual harassment and assault. The biggest challenge facing women in the workplace is something outside of our control, and something the industry needs to address on a whole, as demonstrated by several high-profile lawsuits in the industry.

Along with sexual harassment, many women in tech also felt a general sense of not being included. 66% of women in tech felt excluded from key social and network opportunities due to gender, 59% felt like they did not receive the same opportunities as male counterparts, and 90% reported sexist behavior during company events and industry conferences.

Barney admits that women in technology can sometimes feel out of place. "Every conference and learning engagement I was surrounded by men. They were very much about the technology, I was very much about the business," she said. "I always found ways to learn from them, but apply it to the actual business value our institution would gain from it. At times, you will feel inferior, out of place and perhaps weaker... find a way to fit in! I used my background in athletics and sports to join conversations."

Showing Up and Standing Out

For Vazquez, being a woman in tech can be a tremendous advantage. "I later worked my way up the ladder at a global software company and transitioned into executive management," she said. "As the only female Sr. VP, I was the only woman around the board room table. I never felt being the sole female was an issue. I always felt the highest level of respect from my peers and superiors. And in fact being the token woman sometimes even felt as an advantage because I brought unique perspective from that of my male counterparts which they seemed to appreciate."

The best way to shrink the women tech talent gap is to encourage more young women to consider technology careers. Sylvestre advises young women to be bold and not let anyone intimidate you. "Be okay with not knowing and okay with having to ask for help and spending a lot of personal time learning and refining your skills. Always volunteer for projects even those you might not have a knowledge set in—it's an opportunity to learn and diversify your skill sets," she said.

Barney advises young women to "be prepared for an exciting job that comes with challenges in such a highly dynamic environment. Be flexible and courageous. Set your goals and steer the course—Be a risk-taker only if you have a thorough understanding of how to mitigate the risk. Don't embark on a new technology because someone else is doing it—Have a PLAN! Surround yourself with experts that know the technology and have a passion for the institutional mission."

At the end of the day, having a diverse workforce isn't just about a company feeling good about itself. McKinsey research indicates that gender-diverse companies outperform by 15%. On top of that, ethnically diverse companies perform 35% better.

According to the report "More diverse companies, we believe, are better able to win top talent and improve their customer orientation, employee satisfaction, and decision making, and all that leads to a virtuous cycle of increasing return. This in turn suggests that other kinds of diversity—for example, in age, sexual orientation, and experience (such as a global mind-set and cultural fluency)—are also likely to bring some level of competitive advantage for companies that can attract and retain such diverse talent."

It's clear the benefits of women and people of color in tech greatly outweigh any costs. With the higher returns that diversity is expected (and proving) to bring, the more tech leaders invest now in diversity and inclusion, the further they'll pull ahead of their non-diverse competitors.

> *"Because we tend to network more easily with those we perceive as similar to us, and because women are underrepresented in positions of power, women are less likely to have the network connections—with high-visibility leaders—that lead to promotion."*

To Advance in Tech, Women Need Better Visibility

Shelley Correll and Lori Mackenzie

In the following viewpoint Shelley Correll and Lori Mackenzie argue that an emphasis should be placed on retaining the women who are already working in technology. The authors identify lack of visibility as a hindrance to women wishing to advance in technology fields, and they offer some suggestions for how to overcome this. Correll is professor of sociology at Stanford University and Director of the Clayman Institute for Gender Research. Mackenzie is co-founder of the Institute's Center for the Advancement in Women's Leadership.

As you read, consider the following questions:

1. Why is it more difficult for women to achieve visibility in tech than in other fields?
2. What aspect of women's typical leadership styles do the authors argue is not appreciated in tech?
3. Do the authors offer a suggestion for how women can overcome managers' perceptions?

Silicon Valley companies are making news these days for their efforts to fix the underrepresentation of women in tech. Many are focused on increasing the pipeline of women studying STEM in high school and college. But pipeline factors are not the only reason for the low numbers of women: Companies are failing to retain the female employees they have. A study by Jennifer Glass and coauthors in 2013 found that women leave STEM fields at dramatically higher rates than women in other occupations. After 12 years, 50% of technical women, predominately in engineering and computer science, had switched to other fields; 20% of other women professionals had done the same.

The highest-profile losses in tech are those at the senior level. These women often are less satisfied with their careers, perceive that they are unlikely to advance at their current organizations, or believe they must change jobs in order to reach the next level. As one technology executive has explained to us, "We have some very capable women in the middle management and junior VP levels, but they leave our firm to advance their careers as they continually get passed over for promotion."

What can companies do to stop the departure of senior women? One critical but overlooked strategy: Make sure that women have the right kind of visibility within the organization.

In 2007 and 2008 the Clayman Institute for Gender Research and the Anita Borg Institute conducted research on approximately

1,800 tech workers in seven high-tech companies, finding that women reported being less likely than their male counterparts to be assigned to high-visibility projects.

Earlier this year we led a thought exercise for 240 senior leaders of a Silicon Valley technology company. We asked them to identify the most-critical factors for success at their level. The group agreed on track record and skills-based factors: a history of delivering results, technical depth of expertise, and the ability to manage a technical team.

We then asked them to name the most-critical factors for promotion to their level. A new top criterion emerged, eclipsing all others: visibility. More than technical competence, business results, or team leadership ability—these leaders agreed—visibility is the most important factor for advancement.

We later observed 36 hours of performance calibration reviews in three companies. In these conversations, senior leaders discussed their up-and-coming employees in order to align their performance ratings across the organization. These ratings determine a person's access to salary increases, promotions, and recognition. We also conducted six focus groups with midlevel and senior leaders to understand how they perceive opportunities for advancement at their companies.

Each study validated the importance of visibility in assessing an employee's performance and potential. In our observations, visibility is a complex interaction of perceived skills (particularly technical and leadership ones), access to stretch assignments, and being known—and liked—by influential senior leaders within informal networks. All three are necessary for advancement.

Across each of these categories, however, we observed gendered dynamics that systematically disadvantaged women in achieving visibility, potentially limiting their opportunities for promotion and keeping them from the senior levels of their organizations.

Visibility of Valued Skills

The visibility of one's technical skills influenced how valuable specific employees were perceived to be. This presented a conundrum for women. Since women were less likely to be represented on high-visibility technical projects, they were also less likely to be seen as having the kind of skill set most valued by leaders. And because women were less likely to been seen as owning those highly valued technical skills, they were less likely to be picked for highly visible groups. For example, women were not always invited to contribute to "blue sky" teams, the groups that companies ask to do the biggest, boldest thinking about new technologies and businesses. As one male manager explained, these high-visibility opportunities were not offered to everyone: "People get hand-picked by senior folks to think about this stuff."

The same pattern happened for leadership skills. During performance reviews, we found that the highest marks were given to employees who fit a narrow definition of leadership that tended to reflect a highly visible style. Terms such as "crushes it" and "kills it" were used to describe top performers. While these highly visible behaviors benefited senior men, senior women were often criticized when exhibiting this approach. Comments such as "she is abrasive and runs over people" were given to women. Because women are more likely to be described as having a collaborative, less visible leadership style, they were less likely to win recognition with these narrow definitions. On the other hand, both men and women were criticized for being understated. One review noted, "He is the most conflict-averse person I have met…this will be a limiter."

Visibility in Assignments

As Herminia Ibarra of INSEAD points out, in order to advance women, companies should focus less on mentorship programs and more on putting women into stretch assignments that build both skills and organizational visibility. Our research suggests that women are less able to access these assignments.

Some of the women in our focus groups described being turned away when they requested big, new opportunities. One explained, "There are times where you are discouraged from taking on a stretch assignment. The manager says, 'This will require extra hours, and you have to think about your family. This is not something for you.' I have had that happen to me, and these were experiences needed for a promotion."

Women also commented on how their "likeability" affected their ability to land choice assignments. They recognized that a penalty could come from being perceived as too "aggressive" at work. "A lot of characteristics for the men are seen as assets but are not liked in women," said one focus group participant. For example, "He is a driver; she is demanding and bossy. He is quick; she is agitated."

Our observations of managers discussing employee performance evaluations revealed clearly gendered patterns: Women were labeled as "aggressive," and criticized for their "communication style." We heard comments like "She's rude" or "She's good, but she's really pushy and has to learn to tone it down." For men, similar "aggressive" behaviors, when noted, were reframed in a positive way. For instance, a male leader called out for having "an ego" was reframed by another manager: "I wouldn't say he has an ego, but he's super confident." Or these behaviors were brushed aside. One leader commented about a male candidate, "The style stuff doesn't matter. He is great, and it is irrelevant."

Visibility in Networks

In addition to being visible for the right skills and the right projects, employees also need to be visible to the right people if they want to advance into senior leadership. In one company where we analyzed a sample of performance evaluations, women were half as likely to be talked about in terms of being known to leaders, and twice as likely to be told they needed to increase their visibility to leadership.

Because we tend to network more easily with those we perceive as similar to us, and because women are underrepresented in positions of power, women are less likely to have the network connections—with high-visibility leaders—that lead to promotion. One senior woman who was highly visible called these connections the "secret sauce of promotions" and said that these connections are built over informal networks: "There is a little club that goes out drinking, and there is a poker group where women don't get invited. A lot of decision making happens there." Another woman noted, "In one of my reviews, I received written feedback: '[Name] needs to network more with visible leaders.' Verbally, I was told it means, 'You need to go have drinks with [this person].'"

Closing the Visibility Gap

How can companies ensure women and men have equal opportunities to build their visibility (and promotability) within the organization? We suggest these steps:

- Question what is valued. Examine your promotion criteria and ask: "Are we defining leadership too narrowly and according to an aggressive management style?"
- Equalize access to assignments. Bring more awareness and transparency around the allocation of high-visibility stretch assignments.
- Open up networks. Create more opportunities for women to connect with senior leaders through high-visibility working groups, Q&A sessions, and inclusive networking events.

By clarifying criteria, making the promotion process more transparent, distributing meaningful assignments equitably, and opening up the right networks for women, we can keep women in tech and build a diverse, talented cohort of leaders.

"It's very hard to eliminate our biases, but we can design organizations to make it easier for our biased minds to get things right."

A Data-Based Approach Is Necessary to Design Bias-Free Organizations

Gardiner Morse

In the following viewpoint, Gardiner Morse interviews Iris Bohnet, Director of the Women and Public Policy Program at the Harvard Kennedy School. Bohnet's most recent book, What Works: Gender Equality by Design, *addresses the problem of gender bias in the workplace. Gardiner and Bohnet discuss some of the issues, such as the reasons diversity training is ineffective and what should take its place, that come up in the book. Bohnet advocates a science and data-based approach to finding and implementing diversity programs, and offers suggestions for how organizations might implement programs and practices that would help reduce gender bias. Morse is senior editor for the Harvard Business Review.*

"Designing a Bias-Free Organization," by Gardiner Morse, Harvard Business School Publishing, July-August 2016. Reprinted by permission.

As you read, consider the following questions:

1. Why would a data-based approach be better than the ones organizations are already using?
2. What form of behavioral design used by orchestras does the author use as an example?
3. What examples does Bohnet give of ways organizations unthinkingly send a message that women aren't meant to be leaders?

I ris Bohnet thinks firms are wasting their money on diversity training. The problem is, most programs just don't work. Rather than run more workshops or try to eradicate the biases that cause discrimination, she says, companies need to redesign their processes to prevent biased choices in the first place.

Bohnet directs the Women and Public Policy Program at the Harvard Kennedy School and cochairs its Behavioral Insights Group. Her new book, *What Works*, describes how simple changes—from eliminating the practice of sharing self-evaluations to rewarding office volunteerism—can reduce the biased behaviors that undermine organizational performance. In this edited interview with HBR senior editor Gardiner Morse, Bohnet describes how behavioral design can neutralize our biases and unleash untapped talent.

HBR: Organizations put a huge amount of effort into improving diversity and equality but are still falling short. Are they doing the wrong things, not trying hard enough, or both?

Bohnet: There is some of each going on. Frankly, right now I am most concerned with companies that want to do the right thing but don't know how to get there, or worse, throw money at the problem without its making much of a difference. Many US corporations, for example, conduct diversity training programs without ever measuring whether they work. My colleague Frank Dobbin at Harvard and many others have done excellent research on the effectiveness of these programs, and unfortunately it looks like they largely don't change attitudes, let alone behavior. I encourage anyone who thinks they have a program that works to actually evaluate and document its impact. This would be a huge service. I'm a bit on a mission to convince corporations, NGOs, and government agencies to bring the same rigor they apply to their financial decision making and marketing strategies to their people management. Marketers have been running A/B tests for a long time, measuring what works and what doesn't. HR departments should be doing the same.

What would a diversity evaluation look like?

There's a great classroom experiment that's a good model. John Dovidio and his colleagues at Yale evaluated the effect of an antibias training program on first and second graders in 61 classrooms. About half the classrooms were randomly assigned to get four weeks of sessions on gender, race, and body type with the goal of making the children more accepting of others who were different from them. The other half didn't get the training. The program had virtually no impact on the children's willingness to share or play with others. This doesn't mean you can't ever teach kids to be more accepting—just that improving people's inclination to be inclusive is incredibly hard. We need to keep collecting data to learn what works best.

So the point for corporations is to adopt this same methodology for any program they try. Offer the training to a randomly selected group of employees and compare their behaviors afterward with a control group. Of course, this would also mean defining success beforehand. For diversity training programs to go beyond just checking the box, organizations have to be serious about what they want to change and how they plan to evaluate whether their change program worked.

What does behavioral science tell us about what to do, aside from measuring success?

Start by accepting that our minds are stubborn beasts. It's very hard to eliminate our biases, but we can design organizations to make it easier for our biased minds to get things right. HBR readers may know the story about how orchestras began using blind auditions in the 1970s. It's a great example of behavioral design that makes it easier to do the unbiased thing. The issue was that fewer than 10% of players in major US orchestras were women. Why was that? Not because women are worse musicians than men but because they were perceived that way by auditioners. So orchestras started having musicians audition behind a curtain, making gender invisible. My Harvard colleague Claudia Goldin and Cecilia Rouse of Princeton showed that this simple change played an important role in increasing the fraction of women in orchestras to almost 40% today. Note that this didn't result from changing mindsets. In fact, some of the most famous orchestra directors at the time were convinced that they didn't need curtains because they, of all people, certainly focused on the quality of the music and not whether somebody looked the part. The evidence told a different story.

So this is good news. Behavioral design works.

Yes, it does. The curtains made it easier for the directors to detect talent, independent of what it looked like. On the one hand, I find it liberating to know that bias affects everyone, regardless of their awareness and good intentions. This work is not about pointing fingers at bad people. On the other hand, it is of course also depressing that even those of us who are committed to equality and promoting diversity fall prey to these biases. I am one of those people. When I took my baby boy to a Harvard day care center for the first time a few years back, one of the first teachers I saw was a man. I wanted to turn and run. This man didn't conform to my expectations of what a preschool teacher looked like. Of course, he turned out to be a wonderful caregiver who later became a trusted babysitter at our house—but I couldn't help my initial gut reaction. I was sexist for only a few seconds, but it bothers me to this day. Seeing is believing. That is, we need to actually see counterstereotypical examples if we are to change our minds. Until we see more male kindergarten teachers or female engineers, we need behavioral designs to make it easier for our biased minds to get things right and break the link between our gut reactions and our actions.

What are examples of good behavioral design in organizations?

Well, let's look at recruitment and talent management, where biases are rampant. You can't easily put job candidates behind a curtain, but you can do a version of that with software. I am a big fan of tools such as Applied, GapJumpers, and Unitive that allow employers to blind themselves to applicants' demographic characteristics. The software allows hiring managers to strip age, gender, educational and socioeconomic background, and other information out of résumés so they can focus on talent only. There's also a robust literature on how to take bias out of the interview process, which boils down to this: Stop going with your gut. Those unstructured interviews where managers think they're getting a feel for a candidate's fit or potential are basically a waste of time. Use structured interviews where every candidate gets the same questions in the same order, and score their answers in order in real time. You should also be thinking about how your recruitment approach can skew who even applies. For instance, you should scrutinize your job ads for language that unconsciously discourages either men or women from applying. A school interested in attracting the best teachers, for instance, should avoid characterizing the ideal candidate as "nurturing" or "supportive" in the ad copy, because research shows that can discourage men from applying. Likewise, a firm that wants to attract men and women equally should avoid describing the preferred candidate as "competitive" or "assertive," as research finds that those characterizations can discourage female applicants. The point is that if you want to attract the best candidates and access 100% of the talent pool, start by being conscious about the recruitment language you use.

What about once you've hired someone? How do you design around managers' biases then?

The same principle applies: Do whatever you can to take instinct out of consideration and rely on hard data. That means, for instance, basing promotions on someone's objectively measured

Walmart Doesn't Deny the Data on Discrimination

Today the US Supreme Court has announced that the female employees of Walmart will not be allowed to bring a class action lawsuit against the company, arguing that it has not been shown that they are a class. It would have been the largest employment discrimination suit in history.

It seems timely, then, to re-post our summary of some of the evidence against Walmart. Women are, on average, paid less, are less likely to be salaried, and hold lower-ranked positions than men. This is true even though there is less turnover among women, meaning that the average female employee has been working at Walmart significantly longer than the average male employee.

The US Supreme Court is hearing arguments in the *Dukes v. Wal-Mart* suit. Wal-Mart is accused of egregious and systematic discrimination against the 1.5 million women who have worked there since 1998. The case isn't based on anecdotal accounts; instead, it's backed up by reams of data. Here is some of it.

Women in hourly and especially salaried jobs make less money than men.

Women are disproportionately in hourly jobs (instead of salaried jobs) in every district examined.

Women make less than men in every district examined.

Women dominate the lowest-paying, lowest-ranked jobs at Walmart, and are a smaller and smaller percentages of the workforce as you go up the pay/rank hierarchy.

And this is true despite the fact that women have lower turnover and have, on average, been working at Walmart significantly longer.

Walmart isn't fighting the data. They're not claiming non-discrimination. Instead, they're arguing that compensation should be restricted to the women directly named in the suit instead of the 1.5 million women who've worked there. In other words, they're hoping that the judge will not grant "class action" status to the case. If he does, it will be the largest class action lawsuit in history.

"The Data Behind the Walmart Gender Discrimination Lawsuit," by Lisa Wade, *The Society Pages*, June 20, 2011.

performance rather than the boss's feeling about them. That seems obvious, but it's still surprisingly rare. Be careful about the data you use, however. Using the wrong data can be as bad as using no data. Let me give you an example. Many managers ask their reports to do self-evaluations, which they then use as part of their performance appraisal. But if employees differ in how self-confident they are—in how comfortable they are with bragging—this will bias the manager's evaluations. The more self-promoting ones will give themselves better ratings. There's a lot of research on the anchoring effect, which shows that we can't help but be influenced by numbers thrown at us, whether in negotiations or performance appraisals. So if managers see inflated ratings on a self-evaluation, they tend to unconsciously adjust their appraisal up a bit. Likewise, poorer self-appraisals, even if they're inaccurate, skew managers' ratings downward. This is a real problem, because there are clear gender (and also cross-cultural) differences in self-confidence. To put it bluntly, men tend to be more overconfident than women—more likely to sing their own praises. One meta-analysis involving nearly 100 independent samples found that men perceived themselves as significantly more effective leaders than women did when, actually, they were rated by others as significantly less effective. Women, on the other hand, are more likely to underestimate their capabilities. For example, in studies, they underestimate how good they are at math and think they need to be better than they are to succeed in higher-level math courses. And female students are more likely than male students to drop courses in which their grades don't meet their own expectations. The point is, do not share self-evaluations with managers before they have made up their minds. They're likely to be skewed, and I don't know of any evidence that having people share self-ratings yields any benefits for employees or their organizations.

But it's probably not possible to just eliminate all managerial activities that allow biased thinking.

Right. But you can change how managers do these things. One message here is to examine whether practices that we thought were gender-neutral in fact lead to biased outcomes. Take the SAT, for example. Your score shouldn't have been affected by whether you're male or female. But it turns out it was. The test once penalized students for incorrect answers in multiple-choice questions. That meant it was risky to guess. Research by Katie Baldiga Coffman of Ohio State University shows that this matters, especially for women. Among equally able test takers, male students are more likely to guess, while female students are more likely to skip questions, fearing the penalty and thus ending up with lower scores. Katie's research reveals that gender differences in willingness to take risk account for about half of the gender gap in guessing. An analysis of the fall 2001 mathematics SAT scores suggests that this phenomenon alone explains up to 40% of the gap between male and female students in SAT scores. The 2016 SAT has been redesigned so that it doesn't penalize for incorrect answers. Taking risk out of guessing means that different appetites for risk taking will no longer affect students' final scores. This can be expected to level the playing field for male and female students. Notice that the new SAT doesn't focus on changing the students' mindsets about risk but instead corrects for different risk tolerances. After all, the test is meant to measure aptitude, not willingness to take risk. Organizations should take a page from this book: Look around and see whether your practices by design favor one gender over the other and discourage some people's ability to do their best work. Do meetings, for example, reward those most willing to hold forth? If so, are there meeting formats you can use that put everyone on an equal footing?

How can firms get started?

Begin by collecting data. When I was academic dean at the Harvard Kennedy School, one day I came to the office to find a group of students camped out in front of my door. They were concerned about the lack of women on the faculty. Or so I thought. Much to my surprise, I realized that it was not primarily the number of female faculty that concerned them but the lack of role models for female students. They wanted to see more female leaders—in the classroom, on panels, behind the podium, teaching, researching, and advising. It turns out we had never paid attention to—or measured—the gender breakdown of the people visiting the Kennedy School. So we did. And our findings resembled those of most organizations that collect such data for the first time: The numbers weren't pretty. Here's the good news. Once you collect and study the data, you can make changes and measure progress. In 1999, MIT acknowledged that it had been unintentionally discriminating against female faculty. An examination of data had revealed gender differences in salary, space, resources, awards, and responses to outside offers. The data had real consequences. A follow-up study, published in 2011, showed that the number of female faculty in science and engineering had almost doubled, and several women held senior leadership positions. Companies can do their own research or turn to consultants for help. EDGE, where I serve as a scientific adviser, is a Swiss foundation and private company that helps organizations across the sectors measure how well they do in terms of gender equality. A firm named Paradigm is another. I came across it when I was speaking with tech firms in Silicon Valley and San Francisco. It helps companies diagnose where the problems are, starting by collecting data, and then come up with possible solutions, often based on behavioral designs.

You said that "seeing is believing." But given the lack of senior female role models in organizations, what else can we do?

About a decade ago we noticed that of all the portraits of leaders on the walls of the Kennedy School, exactly zero were of women. The portraits we display affect what our employees and our students believe possible for themselves. I can attest that it was not our intention to signal to fully half of our students that they were not made to be leaders. Rather, this was done unthinkingly. Since then we have added new portraits, including Ida B. Wells, the US civil rights activist and suffragist, and Ellen Johnson Sirleaf, the president of Liberia, winner of the Nobel Peace Prize, and a graduate of the Kennedy School.

You argue that it's often a waste of time to try to debias people—but hanging portraits of women seems like a strategy to actually change individuals' perceptions.

I am not arguing that mindsets can never change. But what we generally find is for beliefs to change, people's experiences have to change first. Being surrounded by role models who look like you can affect what you think is possible for people like you. Sapna Cheryan of the University of Washington, for example, has shown that decorations in a computer science classroom can affect performance. Replacing the male-dominated Star Wars and Star Trek images with gender-neutral art and nature pictures strengthened female students' associations between women and careers in computer science. In another study, women who were shown a picture of Hillary Clinton or Angela Merkel before giving a public speech did objectively better than those who were shown a picture of Bill Clinton or no picture at all. So what do we do with our boardrooms and hallways that celebrate our (male focused) history? When asked this question at a recent talk I gave at the Organization for Economic Cooperation and Development, I answered that, sometimes, we have to "hurry history." I think that presidents John and John Quincy Adams, spouse and son of the thought leader and First Lady, Abigail Adams, would be proud that her portrait now is on Harvard's walls—and of course, its presence makes a big difference to our female students.

Men may resist organizational changes favoring women because they view gender equality as zero sum—if women win, men lose. How then do you enlist men as agents of change?

Few men oppose the idea of benefiting from the entire talent pool—at least in theory. But some are concerned about actually leveling the playing field. In practice, of course, the blind auditions in orchestras have increased competition for male musicians. And the inclusion of women affects competition for men in all jobs. I understand that increased competition can be painful, but I am too much of an economist to not believe in the value of competition. There is no evidence that protectionism has served the world well.

Enlisting men is partly about helping them to see the benefits of equality. Fathers of daughters are some of the strongest proponents of gender equality, for obvious reasons, so they can be particularly powerful voices when it comes to bringing other men along. Research on male CEOs, politicians, and judges shows that fathers of daughters care more about gender equality than men without children or with only sons. I would urge fathers of daughters to be outspoken in their own organizations and to advocate for equality not just as a broad goal, but to actively help drive the changes I describe here—collecting baseline organizational data, promoting experiments, measuring what works, changing processes to limit the impact of our biased minds and level the playing field, and so on. A big part is, simply, continued awareness building—not just of the problem but also of the solutions available to organizations. I recently gave a talk on Wall Street to an audience that was male. I started by inviting people with children to raise their hands. Then I asked those with daughters to raise their hands. Many hands were up. I told them that this made my job easy as some of my biggest allies were in the room. It broke the ice, especially when I told the audience that my husband and I only have sons—who are great feminists, I might add, and in small ways have already brought behavioral insights to their school by reminding the principal to refer to teachers in general as both "he" and "she."

> "The 20/23/34% gender pay gap myth
> for doing the exact same work is a
> statistical fraud that keeps getting
> recycled and promoted by politicians
> because it apparently has a huge
> political payoff for uniformed voters."

The Gender Pay Gap Isn't Backed Up by the Facts

Mark J. Perry

In the following viewpoint, Mark J. Perry argues that, contrary to prevailing opinions supported by data, at least one aspect of women's inequality, the pay gap, is not valid. He opens the viewpoint by stating that the pay gap is not real, then goes on to offer examples of why he thinks it is not. The author cites data about the number of women in leadership positions to support his claims. Perry is a professor of economics at the University of Michigan's Flint campus.

As you read, consider the following questions:

1. What "holiday" does the author use to begin his viewpoint?
2. Name one example the author lists where gender pay discrimination would not be found?
3. What does the author say keeps "the myth" alive?

"Evidence of employers paying women 20% less than men for the exact same work is as elusive as Bigfoot sightings," by Mark J. Perry, American Enterprise Institute, March 27, 2017. Reprinted by permission.

We're just about a week away from the feminist holiday event known as "Equal Pay Day," which will occur next Tuesday on April 4. That annual event brings awareness to a completely bogus apples-to-oranges comparison in incomes by gender. Specifically this year's Equal Pay Day will publicize the 20% unadjusted difference in median annual earnings for women and men in 2015 (most recent data available) when absolutely nothing relevant is controlled for that would explain that 20% raw differences in income like hours worked, marital status, number of children, education, occupation, number of years of continuous uninterrupted job experience, etc.

To start, let me observe that there is widespread acceptance by the general public, especially among women, progressives and Democrats, of the completely bogus claim that women are paid "77 cents on the dollar for doing the same work as men" in the words of President Obama in 2012 (that claim was rated "Mostly False" by Politifact, but is still widely accepted). Hillary Clinton repackaged the bogus claim for the campaign trail by stating in 2015 that "On average, women need to work an extra two hours each day to earn the same paycheck as their male co-workers." The National Committee on Pay Equity (NCPE) claims that because women make only 79.6 cents for every dollar men make, the average American working woman will have to continue work until Tuesday, April 4 — Equal Pay Day — to earn the same amount of income as her male counterpart earned last year. A Tuesday is always selected for Equal Pay Day because that day allegedly represents how far into each work week all year that women have to work to earn what their male co-workers earned during the previous week.

In 2015, Linda Hallman, who was then the executive director of the American Association of University Women (AAUW), sent a mass email about Equal Pay Day saying "Think about it: Women have to work almost four months longer than men do to earn the same amount of money for doing the same job. What's more, we have to set aside a day each year just to call the nation's attention to it."

An October 2016 report from the World Economic Forum ("The Global Gender Gap Report 2016") claims that it will take 170 years—until 2186—to close the "world economic gender gap" based on current trends. A few weeks ago, Louisiana Governor John Bel Edwards and First Lady Donna Edwards hosted the Louisiana Equal Pay Summit in Baton Rouge to promote the governor's commitment to advancing equal pay for women and families throughout Louisiana. Louisiana has the biggest gender pay gap of any US state (66%), and Mrs. Edwards said that "When women bring home a paycheck that is only 66 percent of what their male counterparts earn, the entire family suffers." (Note: Using unadjusted, raw aggregate pay data the same way that it is used by the National Committee on Pay Equity, AAUW, Obama, Hillary Clinton, etc. to make claims of gender discrimination, women working in Gov. Edwards office make just 82 cents for each dollar earned by men).

Despite the widespread acceptance of the frequent "66/77/80 cents on the dollar for the same job" claims documented above, there is rarely ever any specific evidence presented showing that specific organizations are in violation of federal law by paying women 20% or more less than men for doing the same job. What politicians like Obama, Clinton, and Edwards, and gender activist organizations like the NCPE and AAUW are really implying is that firms and organizations across the country are rampantly and illegally violating the Equal Pay Act of 1963 by paying women 66/77/80 cents on the dollar for doing the same work as men, and those deliberate, flagrant and ongoing violations are somehow going undetected. If there were such ubiquitous gender wage disparities in violation of federal law, why are there not extensive investigations by the Department of Justice, the Office of Civil Rights, the US Equal Employment Opportunity Commission, or by Governor Edwards' office? And why isn't there a cottage industry of law firms specializing in representing women who are victims

EVEN ON EBAY

A study of more than 1 million auctions on the online commerce site eBay finds that women receive consistently less money than men for selling the very same products.

Researchers found that when the seller of these popular items was self-identified as female, the auction got fewer bids and a lower final price. For used items, the gender gap was small, with female sellers getting 3% less money on average. But for new products, women received only 80 cents for every dollar that men got for auctioning a similar product on eBay, the team reports today in Science Advances. The reputation scores of the sellers could not account for that difference, nor could any of the auction options such as the "buy it now" or initial prices. The most striking example was gift cards—vouchers for a fixed amount of money that can be spent at certain stores—for which the gender gap persisted, even though the value is obviously the same no matter the seller.

"Even on eBay, Women Get Paid Less for Their Labor," by John Bohannon, American Association for the Advancement of Science, February 19, 2016.

of the supposed pervasive gender discrimination, the way there are hundreds of law firms representing mesothelioma victims who were exposed to asbestos on the job in previous decades?

Just where do we find these companies that apparently have illegal dual-wage policies: one wage schedule for men and another one for women at wages 20/23/34% below their male co-workers for doing the same job? Which specific organizations are actually paying women 20/23/34% less than men and exposing their organizations to legal prosecution, fines and penalties? Those questions are never answered by Obama, Clinton, Gov. and Mrs. Edwards, NCPE or AAUW.

Well, let's next consider some examples of cases where it's pretty clear that we would NOT find the kind of blatant gender pay discrimination that would result in women earning "66/77/80 cents on the dollar for doing the same work as men." Here are some of those examples:

1. Women-owned businesses. According to this report, there are more than 9.1 million women-owned businesses in the United States, employing nearly 8 million workers, which represents more than 7% of all private sector jobs. It seems highly unlikely that women would engage in the highly illegal (and unethical) activity of paying their female employees 20/23/34% less than their male co-workers. If the implication of "77 cents on the dollar" is that women are being victimized by employers, we wouldn't accuse women of being the victimizers of other women, would we? Not likely.

2. Female CEOs. According to the BLS, there were more than 450,000 women holding the position of "Chief Executive" of their organization last year. Would these female CEOs have any tolerance for an illegal company compensation policy that paid female employees 20/23/34% less than their male co-workers for the same job? Not at all likely.

3. Union Members. In 2016, there were more than 14.6 million wage and salary workers represented by unions. Unions typically negotiate compensation contracts based on seniority, not gender, and it would be almost impossible that unions would violate federal law by negotiating contracts with employers that called for paying women 20/23/34% less than men for the same position with the same seniority.

4. Workers Paid by Commission. There are more than 1.2 million real estate agents in the US who are paid by commission, and 55.5% of them are women. There are 630,000 insurance sales agents and nearly half (46.5%) of them are female. When compensation for these sales agents is primarily determined by commission, and those commissions are based on some percentage of sales volume, there doesn't seem to be much support for any claims of a 20% gender pay gap for those occupations. For example, when have you ever heard that "female realtors or insurance agents are paid 80 cents on the dollar for selling the same amount of real estate or insurance as their male colleagues"? Just what I thought—never.

5. Government Employees. There are more than 22.3 million Americans who work for the government at the federal (2.8 million), state (5.1 million), and local level (14.4 million). Illegal discrimination by paying a female government employee 20% less than a man for doing the same government job? Not likely at all. Government salaries are strictly determined by job classification, experience, and seniority, and are clearly not adjusted by gender.

6. Waiters and Waitresses. There are more than 2 million waiters and waitresses in America, and 70% are female. Because their compensation is based primarily on tips, I don't think there could be any case made that "waitresses are paid 20% less on average than waiters for doing the same job, working the same number of hours, serving the same number of customers that generated the same dollar amount of sales." Unless, of course, customers discriminate against women and give waitresses tips that are 20% lower than the tips they leave for waiters? Not likely.

7. Public School Teachers and College Professors. There are nearly 5 million teachers at the elementary and secondary level (mostly at public schools), and another 1.4 million college professors (BLS data here). There are also nearly one million education administrators and almost two-thirds (65.1%) of those positions are held by females. Of course, some of these educators might also be represented in "Union Members" and "Government Employees" categories above, but when have you ever heard a female elementary school teacher or female college professor claim that they were being paid 23% less than their equally-qualified male colleagues? Never. Most of those salary records are public, like for the faculty and staff employed by the University of Michigan (all three campuses). If any female faculty or staff members at the University of Michigan are getting paid 20% (or some other percentage) less than their male counterparts, it should be pretty easy to prove it. A complaint of gender pay discrimination in Michigan can easily be filed here at the website of the Detroit office of the EEOC.

8. Human Resource Professionals. There are about 287,000 human resource managers in the US, and almost 75% of them are female. Would it be even remotely possible that any of the nearly quarter-million female HR managers are engaged in illegal activity and violating federal law by paying other women in their organizations 20/23/34% less than men for the same position? Not likely.

9. Many Large Companies Have Females as Their Top HR Executive. For example, the top HR position at the Target Corporation is held by a woman—Stephanie Lundquist, she's the Executive Vice President and Chief Human Resources Officer, and five of Target's top 11 executives are female. Any possibility that Target is violating the Equal Pay Act, exposing its organization to possible lawsuits, penalties and fines by paying female Target employees 20/23/35%, or even 5% less than men for the same job? Nope. Likewise, Walmart's top two HR executives are women. Any possibility that those female HR executives would tolerate systematic illegal and unethical gender pay discrimination that would result in Walmart paying women 20% less than men and thereby expose the organization to lawsuits and investigations by the Office of Civil Rights and EEOC? Not very likely.

Of course, the list above is not exhaustive and does not completely cover all industries, all occupations, and all female workers, but it should challenge the narrative that women are routinely paid 20 or 23 or 34% less than men—across the board in all industries and for every occupation, even in firms owned or managed by women, or whose HR departments are headed by a woman.

So just where are the organizations that have illegal dual-pay schedules that compensate women 23% less than men for the same job? In reality, those organizations are as rare as a sighting of Bigfoot or the Loch Ness monster. And shouldn't the nearly complete absence of any actual documented cases of individual women being paid 23% less than men for doing the same job lead us to reject the "66/77/80 cents on the dollar" myths once and for all? Apparently not. The myth just keeps getting recycled over and over again, and regularly repackaged by President Obama, Hillary Clinton and Governor Edwards and others—for obvious political purposes. The fact that the myth is clearly unsupported by any actual evidence doesn't seem to matter to most women, nor to nearly all Democrats.

Perversely perhaps, maybe the false "77 cents on the dollar" narrative is actually kept alive by the total lack of any evidence that there are any employers who actually pay women 23% less than men for the same job. After all, it's better to keep those mythical violations very vague, ambiguous, and undocumented as a way to keep the myth alive, like very rare sightings of Bigfoot. If the bogus myth of widespread 23% gender wage gaps throughout the economy was ever exposed to the sunlight of evidence and truth, it would wilt and disappear, no longer available as a popular issue to generate political support and votes from women.

So maybe it's just the distant hope that someday there could be actual evidence of an organization paying women 20% less than men for doing the same work, or that there could someday be a sighting of Bigfoot, that keep those myths alive.

Bottom Line: If there are actually employers who are illegally paying women 20% less than men for doing the same job, those companies should be exposed, publicized and prosecuted. Just like if the Loch Ness monster and Bigfoot do actually exist, they should be exposed and publicized with video footage. But just like the elusiveness of actual evidence for Bigfoot and the Loch Ness monster should make us question their existence, the elusiveness of any widespread evidence of "77 cents on the dollar for doing the same work as men" should also make us question that unsubstantiated gender pay gap myth.

The 20/23/34% gender pay gap myth for doing the exact same work is a statistical fraud that keeps getting recycled and promoted by politicians because it apparently has a huge political payoff for uniformed voters. And it will continue to have a political payoff as long as average Americans, especially women, buy the statistical snake-oil promoted by Democrats that women are paid 20/23/34%

less than men on average for doing the same job. Along with the myths of Bigfoot and the Loch Ness monster, the 23% wage gap claim is a myth that just won't die, regardless, or maybe because of, the scant evidence.

Update: As CD regular "Give Me Freedom" pointed out in the comments on my original post, it's even worse than I suggest because the "77 cents on the dollar" myth as stated is the average gender pay gap and there would obviously be many women who are paid even less than "77 cents on the dollar" for the average to work out to 77 cents. Here's more from GMF:

> So where are the women earning 70, or 60 or 50 cents on the dollar for doing the same work as men, for the average to work out to be 77 cents? If such a large number of women are being paid the same as men, or even close to the same, and the average is 77 cents on the dollar, then there must be a good number of women who are earning much less than 77 cents on the dollar for doing the same work as a man.

I would think we would see and help those women first because their discrimination is even more severe than the average. Just as the "bigger" Bigfoots would be easier to spot, these women who are earning even less than 77 cents on the dollar for doing the same work as men would stand out more and would be more likely to be highlighted as examples of discriminatory pay practices.

*"Women wouldn't feel such a need
to side with men were they equal
to men. Unfortunately, this is not
the case."*

US Voters Still Prefer Male Candidates

Francesco Maria Morettini

In the following excerpted viewpoint, Francesco Maria Morettini argues that the 2016 US presidential election proved that the country is not ready for a woman president, even if she is vastly overqualified in comparison. During the election, Donald Trump made no secret of his sexist, misogynist views, yet nearly half the voters in the nation voted for him. Morettini points out that both candidates, Hillary Clinton and Trump, attempted to highlight certain of their personality traits that are generally considered masculine, suggesting that voter may desire masculine traits in their leaders. Morettini is a master's candidate at the University of Oxford.

As you read, consider the following questions:

1. What did the Pew survey cited in the viewpoint reveal?
2. How did Clinton respond to Trump's attempts to feminize her according to this viewpoint?
3. What theory does the author suggest to explain the fact that so many women voted for Trump?

"The man behind the new president," by Francesco Maria Morettini, Observer Research Foundation, November 14, 2016. Reprinted by permission.

E ven though the US political system seems to reflect traditional gender stereotypes, the majority of Americans seem to believe that women and men make equally good political leaders: "women are every bit as capable of being good political leaders as men." This seems to directly defy the patriarchal mentality that sees women as unfit for political office. Yet, when it comes to choosing candidates, people still cling to gender stereotypes that give rise to a consistent gender gap in opinions about the strengths of male and female political leaders. In a 2014 survey conducted by PEW, 41 percent of women and 27 percent of men believe that women are better at working out compromises, and are more honest and ethical. Whilst the patriarchal nature of politics can be challenged by arguing that these 'feminine' characteristics may give an advantage to women for politics, the survey suggests that women and men play an active role in reinforcing the stereotypes associated to their own gender.

Moreover, whilst there is a widespread belief that men have an easier path to political leadership (link), American men and women differ in their opinions regarding whether US politics is structured around patriarchy and masculinity. In another PEW survey, the majority of American women (63 percent) believe that women still face obstacles, whilst the majority of American men (58 percent) are of the opinion that gender barriers are largely gone. Hence in the US, social awareness of patriarchy is still gendered—women are largely aware of gender barriers, whereas the majority of men aren't. Overall, 45 percent of Americans believe that the obstacles faced by women are now largely gone. This partial blindness to patriarchy is a result of patriarchy itself, and has deeply influenced the current elections. In previous polls, the majority of those who believe that women face obstacles in politics were likely to vote for Clinton, whilst those that are blind to this were more likely to vote for Trump.

Donald Trump has not ceased to surprise us with his masculine, sexist and misogynistic attitude. By calling women "dogs" and "slobs," by bragging about the size of his penis, flaunting his testosterone score on Dr. Oz and by downplaying the importance of his sexually aggressive comments about married women as simple "locker-room talk," Trump actively sought to establish his manhood in order to profit from the patriarchal, masculine structure of the political system. He is not trying to be a man, but the man: Trump has sought to elevate himself to the level of the hegemonic, supreme masculine man that embodies to "perfection" all the above mentioned characteristics of masculinity.

Sociologist Connell has argued that "men cannot hold state power without having become, collectively, the agents of violence" (2005, p248). The aggressive stance utilised by Trump is reflective of this; his impetuousness and thoughtlessness end up being rewarded by his electors, rather than punished. Many of Trump voters have said that they do not care about his sexually aggressive comments, as Trump tells it like it is. The results of the elections are a clear indication of this.

Trump's attempts to cement his masculine attitudes derive from the fact that many voters prefer voting for a candidate who is a "man." It has been demonstrated that American voters conflate competent leadership with masculine traits, and that sociopolitical imagination is shaped and limited by masculinity (Hutchings, 2008, p23). This means that Trump's masculine, aggressive stance has resonated among working-class white men "who feel emasculated by economic disruption and changing gender roles."

This election coincides with a moment of socioeconomic and political distress, and political scientists are aware that in cases like this voters turn to men, who are vigorous, project resolution and call for action. When interviewing Trump supporters, political commentator David Frum explains that Trump's appeal to millennial men rests on the fact that voters "feel [that] masculine traits are devalued... [they] have never seen a man's man in politics before." In short, Americans who most dislike Clinton (and are therefore likely to vote for Trump) are those who most fear emasculation and those who "completely agree" that society is becoming too feminine and soft. In asking voters why they would be voting for Trump, respondents have said that they appreciate his "aggressiveness, strength, and boldness," adding that if Hillary Clinton will be elected, the "idea... that leadership is a man's job" will be lost. This exemplifies the influence of patriarchy and masculinity on the mental constructions of many American voters. Such an influence is so profound to lead to the victory of Donald Trump.

When trying to affirm his masculinity, Trump did not limit himself to showing it. He also actively tried to feminise Clinton in order to demonstrate that she lacks the masculine characteristics desired for political leadership since she is a woman. This was not a new phenomenon; candidates have long been feminised by their opponents to profit from the unconscious incongruence between femininity and presidential leadership; moreover, this is a strategy used to reinforce masculinity itself (Enloe in Hutchings, 2008, p26). For instance, he repeatedly criticised her on her lack of presidential qualities, often questioning her strength and stamina. He also objectified her by arguing that "she doesn't have the looks [for presidency]." Trump's strategy to portray Clinton in what are considered to be feminine traits goes hand in hand with the finding that those presidential candidates who are portrayed as more feminine in media coverage are more likely to lose the election.

Mental constructions of patriarchy and masculinity are so deeply embedded in the mind of some voters that a group of Trump supporters have produced a number of overtly sexist pins to advocate for Trump's election. Nothing is surprising about them—neither their lack of concrete reasons to vote for Trump, nor the fact that they have to revert to patriarchy and masculinity in order to garner some votes. Pins display writings like: "Don't be a pussy. Vote for Trump in 2016"; "Trump 2016: Finally someone with balls." There are also T-shirts saying "Trump that bitch" and "Hillary sucks but not like Monica."

Even the campaigners that are trying to undermine Trump's candidacy have adopted strategies that are influenced by conceptions of masculinity. Statues portraying Donald Trump without balls have been erected in cities such as NY, Cleveland,

San Francisco and LA. Their aim was to conduct an assault to Trump's masculinity, to show how fake his 'manhood' is. The statues do, however, show that installation is premised on the conviction that feminised men are less fit to lead. "Trump without his balls unwittingly elevates masculinity in the presidential contest at the expense of femininity."

For a few moments during the campaign, however, it seemed like masculinity wouldn't necessarily help Trump. After the release of the video containing Trump's lewd sexual remarks, a growing list of Republicans, both women and men, withdrew their support for Trump. House speaker Paul Ryan stated that he was 'sickened' by Trump's comments. A group of Senators and House members withdrew support for him with some demanding that he step aside. The list of party figures publicly rejecting Mr. Trump include many prominent elected officials, such as Senator John McCain of Arizona, the 2008 nominee. Even Mr. Pence, the Vice President, stated that he was "offended by the words and actions described by Donald Trump" in the video. And Obama has urged senior Republicans to shun him.

A possible explanation given at the time could be that Trump's masculinity would not be sustainable in the long term, but would still help him win some votes in the short term. Trump has been trying to naturalise his masculinity by adopting an arrogant, lewd and misogynist attitude that denigrates, sexualises and objectifies women, such as Clinton. This is a type of masculinity (Enloe, in Hutchings, 2008, p26), which was believed not to be tolerated in the current US political scene, as the growing list of Republicans shunning Trump seemed to show. But the results of the elections speak clearly: electors have preferred Trump as President, exactly in virtue of his arrogant, sexist, misogynistic and masculine attitude.

Clinton was aware that Trump's displays of masculinity could not be widely tolerated; consequently, she tried to further demonstrate that Trump's type of masculinity is not suitable for the presidential office. In the first two presidential debates, she repeatedly attracted people's attention to the sexist comments made by Trump, such as that "pregnancy is an inconvenience to employers," or that "women don't deserve equal pay unless they do as good a job as men." The Clinton campaign also released a video, just after the first presidential debate, featuring former Miss Universe Alicia Machado testifying that Trump had shamed her for gaining weight, leading her to develop an eating disorder.

At the same time, Clinton also adopted a more masculine attitude in order to better fit the patriarchal requirements for the US presidency. Her desire to appear tougher and more assertive resulted in her adopting a more masculine way of speaking. Political science researcher Jennifer Jones has analysed Clinton's speech patterns and has discovered that Clinton has come to speak in an increasingly masculine way. That is, she increasingly took up speech patterns such as first person plural words (the royal "we"), articles, prepositions, words with more than six letters and words associated with anger, which are generally associated with men's speech. Hence, she argues that Clinton has conformed to the practices that women adopt to achieve power and influence in a profession still dominated by men and male models—"the powerful voice in politics still speaks with a masculine style."

Clinton also tried to get the best of both worlds. As well as behaving in a masculine way, she also made sure to be feminine enough to appeal to an even wider electorate. During her 2008 presidential campaign, gender issues were considered a disadvantage for the elections. It was conflictual for her to acknowledge her identity as a woman and to establish herself as a competent politician. For this reason, she deliberately underplayed her female identity and her candidature was devoid of any reference to gender-related matters. During the current elections, however, Clinton put women's issues at the centre of the debate. She strongly emphasised child care, paid family and equal pay. She no longer had to underplay gender issues in order to be seen as a serious contender for the presidency.

Still, in a poll before the elections, only four percent of Clinton voters have said they would support her because she is a woman.

Furthermore, during the primaries, many feminists preferred siding with Bernie Sanders, rather than with Clinton herself. Sanders obtained 53 percent of the female vote overall, compared with Clinton's 46 percent. When we consider women under 30, 82 percent of them voted for Sanders. This could mean that Clinton's attempt to appeal to women's votes and to those electors that stand up for issues like equal pay and child care may have not completely hit the mark. She may be a woman, but not feminist enough. Is she too masculine? Is she part of the establishment that has done psychological, environmental, and economic damage to the US?

Exit data polls collected by The *New York Times* seem to demonstrate this latter point. Clinton was not elected because she is a woman, and women did not vote for her either. Whereas black and Latino women mostly voted for Clinton, the majority of white women voted for Trump. This comes as a shocking surprise, given the denigration and the poor consideration that Trump has had for women in the past. Trump's success is entirely white and working-class, and has been ensured by those very women that have been subordinated and marginalised by the very own patriarchal rhetoric that Donald Trump has adopted.

A Battle of the Sexes

As well as being an ideological, policy based battle, this presidential campaign seems to have been a battle of the sexes. Pre-election polls show that among those that believe that women still face obstacles for political progress, 70 percent would vote for Clinton. Contrarily, the majority of people who would vote for Trump do not believe that women face obstacles in life. On a similar note, a study has shown that voters with masculine personality types were more likely to support Republicans, whilst voters with more feminine traits were more likely to support Democrats. The result is a split electorate: those who are blind to the patriarchal structure of politics were likely to have voted for Trump; those who witness the daily masculinisation of the US political realm and daily life were likely to have voted for Clinton.

The news that the majority of white women (53 percent) voted for Trump seems to undermine this "battle of the sexes" idea, as it is clear that the majority of women have played an active role in supporting Trump's white supremacy. Why? Some point to women's self loathing, or hypocrisy, or even the overtly racist belief that white supremacy should be privileged over any other issue. But most of all, women's decision to vote for Trump is indicative of the fact that women want to be like men. And thus, they have behaved like the majority of men, who have voted for Trump. Women wouldn't feel such a need to side with men were they equal to men. Unfortunately, this is not the case.

The fact remains that white women have preferred voting for a candidate who has consistently reduced women to their sexual attributes and has tried "to pit straight white men against everyone else—women, people of colour, people in the LGBTQ community, immigrants."

These elections have seemed to be all apart from presidential. Half of Clinton's supporters said they would back her so as to keep Trump from winning. Clinton's central message also seemed to be that everyone had to step up and stop Donald Trump from being president, rather than stepping up to make her president. These elections were actually a referendum on Donald Trump.

Trump undertook a clever political strategy so as to take advantage of the patriarco-masculine structure of politics. He clearly tried to further masculinise himself and to feminise Clinton. On her part, Clinton sought to further masculinise Trump, to show how unfit for politics his type of masculinity is; but this hasn't worked. At the same time, she exploited both her masculine and feminine traits in order to gain more votes. The two sides have fought fiercely; but what the results demonstrate is that the gender gap is real, and that women themselves have contributed to cement it.

What Trump's election show is that electors still prefer a man to a woman, even though that man has been charged with sexual rape accusations, displays a visible gender-bias, is sexist and misogynistic. This blatantly demonstrates that the patriarchal and masculine nature of American politics has won. These elections have been a contest for competing notions of manhood (Katz, 2016), where the display of characteristics associated with hegemonic masculinity is still one of the major factors to influence a candidate's eligibility to the presidential office. Masculinity still helps candidates look more confident and competent; that has certainly helped Trump win the election. And white women have given masculinity a further boost.

Periodical and Internet Sources Bibliography

The following articles have been selected to supplement the diverse views presented in this chapter.

Mark Bergen and Ellen Huet, "Google Fires Author of Divisive Memo on Gender Differences." *Bloomberg Technology*, August 7, 2017. https://www.bloomberg.com/news/articles/2017-08-08/google-fires-employee-behind-controversial-diversity-memo

Soraya Chemaly, "The Scariest Thing About Donald Trump's Misogyny Is That It's Not Unusual At all." *Quartz*, June 5, 2016. https://qz.com/698404/the-scariest-thing-about-donald-trumps-misogyny-is-that-its-not-unusual-at-all/

Madeline Farber, "3 Reasons Why the Gender Pay Gap Still Exists." *Fortune*, April 3, 2017. http://fortune.com/2017/04/03/equal-pay-day-2017-wage-gap/

Sukjong Hong. "What Gender Gap? Exit Polls Show White Women Actually Preferred Trump to Clinton." *New Republic*. https://newrepublic.com/minutes/138601/gender-gap-exit-polls-show-white-women-voters-actually-preferred-trump-clinton

Amy Jadesimi, "The Glass Ceiling Is Cracked, Not Broken." *Forbes*, August 8, 2016. https://www.forbes.com/sites/amyjadesimi/2016/08/08/female-leadership-the-glass-ceiling-is-cracked-not-broken/#457f67dd698b

Sarah Kliff, "The Truth about the Gender Wage Gap." *Vox*, September 8, 2017. https://www.vox.com/2017/9/8/16268362/gender-wage-gap-explained

Nancy LeTourneau, "Yes, We Still Need to Talk about the Patriarcy." *Washington Monthly*, August 11, 2017. https://washingtonmonthly.com/2017/08/11/yes-we-still-need-to-talk-about-patriarchy/

Liza Mundy. "Why Is Silicon Valley So Awful to Women?" *The Atlantic*, April 2017. https://www.theatlantic.com/magazine/archive/2017/04/why-is-silicon-valley-so-awful-to-women/517788/

CHAPTER 3

Has Feminism Changed Things for Women?

Chapter Preface

Despite all the inequality discussed so far in this resource, it is clear that women have made a lot of progress over the years. Anyone who doubts that needs to take a quick trip back in time— and we don't have to travel very far. Women were not allowed to apply for credit until 1974. Until 1978, women could be fired if they became pregnant. Marital rape was not criminalized in all 50 states until 1993. It was not until 1993 that women senators were allowed to wear pants on the Senate floor.

In 2017, only 5.4 percent of Fortune 500 companies had women CEOs. In 1995, there were none. And, of course, despite her loss in the general election, Hillary Clinton, pantsuit and all, made history in 2016 by becoming the first female presidential candidate to be nominated by a major political party. (And also the first female candidate to win a majority of the popular vote.)

Yet, for all that progress, women still face an astonishing amount of obstacles, both social and economic, when it comes to achieving equality with males. While some of these issues seem more symbolic than practical (wearing pants, for example), or at least the consequences of the discrimination don't seem so dire, others are far more serious. And it is in the weightier issues where women have made the least progress, particularly poor women and women of color. Women are increasingly heads of households, yet they often do not have the income or the social support of men heads of households. Women have had the vote since 1920, yet they still make up barely over 20 percent of the legislative bodies worldwide. (This may be rapidly changing in many nations, including the United States and Canada.)

The viewpoints in this chapter take a look at how things have changed for women in the past few decades, and how they have not. The selections here examine women's progress, or lack of progress, in business, academia, the media, the internet, and the streets. They offer insight, suggestions, and in a few cases, alarms, for today's wave of feminists and activists.

| "Students studying sociology now take it for granted that gender is central to sociological analysis."

Women's Studies Programs Have Brought Attention to Women's Concerns

Stevi Jackson

In the following viewpoint, Stevi Jackson argues that one way in which things have changed for women in recent years, is that they now have their own academic discipline, and perhaps more importantly, other academic disciplines, such as sociology and psychology, are less focused primarily on men. The author recounts the growth and evolution of women's studies programs (now more often called gender studies programs) in universities, and how those disciplines have changed the conversation about women's roles and place in society. Jackson is a professor at the Centre for Women's Studies at the University of York in the UK.

As you read, consider the following questions:

1. When were the UK's first women's studies programs set up?
2. What accounts for the decline in these programs?
3. Why did universities change the name of the programs to gender studies?

"Women's Studies, Gender Studies and Feminism," by Stevi Jackson, Discover Society, March 1, 2016. Reprinted by permission.

Women's studies as an academic enterprise had its roots in second wave feminism and originated as a challenge to male-defined and male-centred knowledge. Students studying sociology now take it for granted that gender is central to sociological analysis. This was not always so. The sociology I was taught as an undergraduate in the late 1960s and early 1970s was the sociology of men as if they represented the whole of society— and primarily white western men. Women featured only briefly, in lectures on family and kinship. This was not a problem peculiar to sociology; women in other disciplines were facing similar biases in relation to what counted as knowledge. Some of us, inspired by feminist ideas, began to complain and then to act.

By the middle of the 1970s feminists began to organise across disciplines as well as within them. Young feminist academics and graduate students met to discuss the possibility of launching women's studies as a new "women-centred way of knowing" that would challenge the prevailing androcentric view of society and culture prevalent in the humanities and social sciences (science subjects weren't even having the debate at that stage). We offered adult education courses in our communities as well as agitating in universities, using the skills we were learning through political activism to make a difference within the academy. At this time most feminist academics were also activists in the wider women's liberation movement. We were a privileged group of women; not all of us were by any means middle class in origin but we had gained a university education at a time when only a small minority of young people did so—and this, perhaps, is partly why second wave feminism is seen as overwhelmingly middle class.

Looking back, we were remarkably successful within a very short period of time. The first women's studies courses, at postgraduate level were set up in the early 1980s, initially at Kent and Bradford, then York, followed by many others. Throughout the 1980s both undergraduate and postgraduate women's studies programmes sprang up in universities and polytechnics across the UK and by the end of the decade we had our own professional association, initially called the Women's Studies Network (later to be renamed the Feminist and Women's Studies Association). In many ways the 1980s were an inauspicious time for new academic initiatives. It was the Thatcher era, with its cuts in central government funding of HE, leading to a lack of academic jobs and thus little opportunity for job mobility. Yet among those who had been recruited into academia before the job slump took hold, there was a critical mass of committed young feminists willing to put considerable effort into developing women's studies. When a group of us in a Polytechnic proposed a women's studies degree we met little opposition. As far as the "authorities" were concerned we could go ahead in seeking validation provided we could do so without any additional resources. What mattered, we were told, was "bums on seats," and provided we could achieve this (and bring in the fees paid by said bums), the powers that be had little interest in what we were teaching. Programmes such as this one were initially successful. At undergraduate level they often attracted mature women students without standard academic qualifications who came in via access courses.

Women's Studies programmes relied heavily on the energy and feminist commitment of, primarily, junior academic staff often on temporary contracts. While these degrees appeared to flourish, under-resourcing and the lack of institutional support also made them rather precarious. During the 1990s a few more job opportunities opened up. One consequence was that when those involved in women's studies moved on, and their replacements often lacked the same expertise or commitment. At the same time cuts in the funding of students, the decline in student grants and their replacement by loans meant many less advantaged women could no longer contemplate a degree course while others opted for "safer" subjects. As student numbers declined in the 1990s and early 2000s, many degree programmes shut down. While there were a few new ones at postgraduate level (usually badged as gender studies), free standing undergraduate degrees gradually disappeared, although a few universities still offer women's or gender studies routes through other degree programmes. Postgraduate courses have, however, proved more durable.

This decline has not meant the demise of feminist knowledge production within universities. The rise of women's studies also led to feminism having an impact on a variety of disciplines, with a gradual "mainstreaming" of feminist research and theory in much of the humanities and social sciences. As feminist knowledge became more academically respectable it was increasingly possible to build a career as an avowedly feminist scholar. This very success, however, has created another problem: a rift between academic feminism and feminist activism, which became apparent in the 1990s. Feminist knowledge, in particular feminist theory, was increasingly more abstract and distant from the everyday challenges facing women in the outside world. There was pressure to keep up with whatever intellectual trend was currently fashionable in order to appear respectably intellectual and "cutting edge." Not all feminist academics played this game, but we were facing other problems that worked against maintaining our connections with activism.

As the generation who founded women's studies became more senior we found ourselves over-burdened by work responsibilities, which was exacerbated by the increasing bureaucratisation of higher education and the audit culture. This left little time or energy for activism. Early career feminist academics were also under pressure. Where my own generation were largely left alone to do whatever research we felt like at the beginning of our careers, as long as we fulfilled our basic teaching commitments, new academics recruits are expected to undertake a teaching qualification, apply successfully for research grants, publish in reputable journals, create impact and be accountable for their intellectual productivity. Yet feminist research and teaching in universities continues to thrive— and not all of it is divorced from activist concerns. Some of it has made, and continues to make, a difference in the "real world," impacting on government and international policies in a number of areas, some of it still making connections with activism.

Do We Still Need Women's Studies?

Most of the surviving programmes in the UK are now branded as gender studies or gender and women's studies. The pragmatic reason for this is that it is seen as less feminist, more respectable and less threatening than women's studies. While the term "gender" was initially used by feminists to establish the social (as opposed to natural) basis of hierarchy and division between men and women, this meaning has largely been lost in its incorporation into everyday language. "Gender," therefore has come to seem a safe and neutral term. "Gender studies" is also seen as more inclusive than "women's studies," taking in men and women as well as those who identify as neither.

Another objection to "women's studies" is the problem with "women" as a category. It has been recognised, since the heyday of women's studies, that "women" is not a unitary category (see e.g. Brah 1991). This is, in my view, not a reason to abandon "women's studies" or the idea of women centred knowledge. Such knowledge can be a focus for exploring differences and inequalities among women. This is, indeed, what we do on the women's studies MA at York. We start from Toril Moi's (2001) question: "what is a woman?" This provides a means of interrogating the category, opening up issues of differences among women and who counts as a woman, which then serves as a base for considering how gender is interlinked with other social inequalities and differences.

One justification for retaining the term "women's studies" is that it prioritises women-centred knowledge and starts from women's varied locations in the world. It also pays homage to the roots of the discipline in feminism's history. There is another important reason. Internationally "women" makes more sense than gender. Gender is, as has long been recognised, an Anglophone concept, one that is not understood globally. Many of our students come from parts of the world where gender is a meaningless term—and they come with a commitment to understanding and addressing the myriad problems women face in their own countries and beyond. If we are serious about working towards a more inclusive feminism, one that is not focused on the relatively privileged societies of the global north, there are good grounds for retaining the name "women's studies."

In practice, there is little that definitively differentiates between gender studies and women's studies in terms of what is taught. To be sure, every curriculum is different, but all, whether women's studies or gender studies, use feminist research and theory, discuss gender and inevitably discuss men as well as women and transgressions of gender binaries. Whether we call what we do women's studies or gender studies or a hybrid of the two, there is reason to celebrate its survival in the harsh academic climate of our times and continue to defend it. But, given that feminism has had such an influence on sociology and other disciplines, do we still need these programmes? I would argue that we do. There are limits to feminism's influence, evident for example in the way some mainstream (or malestream) academics continue to ignore feminist scholarship even where it is of obvious relevance. There is still a need for an institutional base, for a public profile that brings women's concerns to the fore in the light of the many problems facing women in the world today.

This brings me back to activism. In the early years of my time in the Centre for Women's Studies at York (in the late 1990s and early 2000s), few of our students had activist backgrounds, and most who did were either overseas students from beyond the Euro-American axis or mature students with second wave affiliations. Today, however, our students are increasingly oriented to activism, to addressing the pressing problems facing women globally and they are wonderfully creative in the forms of activism they pursue. In this I see hope—both for women's studies/gender studies in the academy and for the impact of feminism in the wider world.

References

Brah, Avtar (1991) "Questions of difference and international feminism," in Jane Aaron and Sylvia Walby (Eds.) *Out of the Margins*, London, Falmer Press.

Moi, Toril (2001) *What Is a Woman? And Other Essays*. Oxford: Oxford University Press.

> *"Be all nicey, nice and you risk losing
> credibility. Be hard-charging and risk
> being called a b---h or booted."*

Progress Has Stalled for Women in the Media

Danna Walker

*In the following excerpted viewpoint, Danna Walker opens with yet
more dire statistics about women in the workplace, in this case in
journalism. The author argues that there is a difference in managing
style between men and women, and asks what women have to do
to succeed in management positions in media. Walker shares her
personal experience in journalism as well as her academic expertise,
as she asserts that we have become complacent about the problem,
and explores some of the reasons progress has stalled for women in
the media. Walker is a journalist and academic.*

As you read, consider the following questions:

1. How does Walker suggest getting past the problem of
   appearing either weak or too aggressive?
2. What, according to Walker, is the role of women
   managers in the news room?
3. Why does Walker say that it is easy for the public to think
   that women are doing better in the media profession than
   they really are?

"Women News Managers Reflect on Leadership Styles in a Changing Industry," by Danna
Walker, Academic and Journalist, author of "Women and Media: The History of an
Activist's Fight for Equity," *American Journalism Review*, August 6, 2014. Reprinted by
permission.

By the Women's Media Center's calculation this year, 36 percent of the journalism workforce is comprised of women, while women make up 23 percent of journalism leadership and earn 25 percent less than men in the same positions. Women do better in middle management, but there is a blockade at that level globally. This is not just in journalism, mind you, but that doesn't make me feel any better.

In top journalism companies, women comprise only 10 percent of the leadership, the center found. In 1982, women made up 10 percent of the leadership positions in newspapers.

When you get to 2012, that climbed to 19 percent (22 percent in television and a dominant 55 percent in social media), but only four women serve as editors-in-chief of the nation's top 25 newspapers, according to the WMC. Such numbers amid turmoil in the industry have created a lot of discussion and efforts at reform, but no one seems to disagree that diversity is lacking. (A new survey by the American Society of News Editors shows minority employment just over 13 percent in newsrooms in 2013, a percentage point higher than the previous year and just short of the record high of 13.73 percent in 2006.)

"We know an unequal workplace is not a new thing," said Barbara Friedman, associate professor at the School of Journalism and Mass Communication at the University of North Carolina and editor of the scholarly journal, *American Journalism*. She focuses on research about women. "We know that groups have been studying this and trying to change this for centuries."

The *New York Times*, itself, has been the focus of much study because of its stature within the industry.

"Studies of the *Times*' book review, the editorial section, the front page, even obituaries have consistently revealed a gender imbalance. Men are represented more often than women as subjects, sources and authors," said Friedman. "The *New York Times* has a very long history in terms of organizational makeup and newspaper content of being imbalanced. And for better or worse, this is the news organization that often sets the course for others."

More than 20 years ago, ASNE set a goal of having news staffs mirror the American population in terms of minority representation by 2000. With that goal blown, it now has set a parity date of 2025.

Women on the Ground

Because women make up 64 percent of graduates in journalism and communication schools and are prevalent in the industry, according to figures compiled by the WMC, the drought of women in leadership may not be so obvious. As a graduate student, I studied the history of women and journalism, uncovering the decades of legal battles, activism, initiative and groundbreaking efforts, including with satellites and other technology used to publish and broadcast alternative feminist media.

But even I got complacent, thinking when I entered academia in 2003 that we were on a forward trajectory, especially with the digital disruption.

As a college professor, I pushed my students to learn new roles and fully embrace the democratizing nature of the new interactivity. The sense that journalism could be open to all and what I saw as the old, patriarchal model turned-upside-down was exhilarating.

When I had a chance in 2010 to enter digital journalism as a manager of journalists working remotely throughout Maryland at AOL Patch, I jumped at it. The news world was changing, and as a recently practicing feminist scholar it was my chance to experiment by bringing those principles to a traditionally male-dominated role in a progressive digital media company.

[…]

I did my best to empower those whom I managed. I often took a page, literally, from Jill Geisler's book, *Work Happy: What Great Bosses Know*, which is as feminist a treatise as I've seen on the practical side of management in journalism. Geisler, who heads Poynter's leadership and management programs and was a moderator at the Poynter forum, preaches collaboration, positive communication and a coaching method of leadership.

"I would make no apologies for the word feminism," Geisler told AJR. "If it's feminist, then it must be organically feminist," based on Geisler's belief that the first priority of a leader is to help other people succeed. "My slogan has always been life's too short to work with jerks," regardless of gender, she said.

I don't want to ascribe certain behaviors to certain genders—I'm talking here about leadership style and the purposeful act of being a positive force and perhaps listening more and trusting talented people. When I was a newsroom manager, my employees were the ones who came up with the best ideas and the most effective solutions. I didn't have all the answers; no manager does.

Rachel Smolkin, who is leaving her job as Politico's managing editor of news to become executive editor of CNN Politics Digital, is looked to as one among a new generation of women leaders in a digital future. She told the panel that it's helpful for women to be aware that the outside world sometimes expects them to smile more and be friendlier and more nurturing—advice she later said she and other women should feel free to ignore in favor of authenticity.

"I think women are just as capable of being mean," she told AJR. "I just try and be honest with the people who work for me. If you don't demonstrate that you have trust and faith in people by letting them do what they do, it doesn't make for a very fun or easy place to work. That takes a lot of strength."

Thinking Like a Man

Feminism is about understanding and disrupting power relations. When you're a manager and you want an excellent product, it's, as Smolkin said, a challenge.

> Be all nicey, nice and you risk losing credibility. Be hard-charging and risk being called a b---h or booted. [...]

Barbara Barnett, associate professor and associate dean in the William Allen White School of Journalism and Mass Communications at the University of Kansas, has studied feminist leadership. She remembers a conversation during her time at a newspaper in which a new female manager had come aboard. The six male managers involved declared that the woman would succeed "because she thinks like a man," Barnett said. "I was stunned. There's already a dichotomy set up. You have to be one of us.

"We've got this idea in corporate America—a vision of what a manager should be. Frankly, sometimes that's being a bully. You can lead without being a bully."

Barnett said that women journalism students see the inequities that women who were pioneers in the field perhaps didn't. As Barnett describes it, these young women still have anxiety about gender and journalism, but maybe they have a perspective that means they'll get leadership right—in the way Smolkin described.

"A female journalism student came to me in tears, 'It really is a man's world.' What am I going to tell her? 'Oh, no, it's not?' I see it every day. The fact that you're in college, the fact that you recognize this, you will be able to take charge of your own destiny. When I was in college it wasn't necessarily clear that I could do that."

For the most part, I feel good about my 3 1/2-year experiment as a feminist news manager. I got positive feedback from some of those I managed. I worked hard at it, but in the heat of breaking stories, I raised my voice a couple of times, and later apologized.

[...]

Smolkin noted Glasser's call for companies to go beyond putting women in high places by supporting them in those roles, particularly when they fail at some things.

"One of the things she talks about is how important it is to support women in these positions so they have the space and freedom to innovate, to experiment and most importantly to make mistakes.... Are you going to withhold your support, say, 'Oh, they're not temperamentally suited for this job'—a term women hear probably more than men, or are you going to stand behind them and back them?" Smolkin told the panel.

Of course, there are exceptions in the media world—Arianna Huffington and Tina Brown come to mind. But for anyone still doubting whether women face particular problems as leaders, Smolkin pointed out Matt Lauer's recent interview with General Motors chief executive Mary Barra, who has decades of experience but who was subjected to questioning on whether she was hired to "soften" GM's image and if she could do the job and also be a good mom—questions not asked of men.

| "*A group of people chipping away, bit by bit, can make a major difference.*"

One Dedicated Feminist Can Make a Huge Difference

Jeff Elder and Ed Erhart

In the following viewpoint, Jeff Elder argues that, not only are women underrepresented in many important areas—they also are subject to harassment by online trolls when they do attempt to represent. The author profiles a young feminist (and medical student) who responded to sexist trolls in a unique and ultimately powerful way, turning what could have been devastating harassment into a force for good. Elder is senior writer and editor in social media for McAfee. Erhart is editorial associate at the Wikimedia Foundation.

As you read, consider the following questions:

1. What is Temple-Wood's Wikipedia editor user name?
2. How many English-language articles does Wikipedia offer, according to the viewpoint?
3. By what percentage have Wikipedia's women's biographies increased?

Almost one year ago today, the Wikimedia blog wrote about Wikipedia editor Emily Temple-Wood and her personal stand against sexist trolls. The post described how Emily, a medical student at Midwestern University who edits as User:Keilana, would create a Wikipedia article about a woman scientist for every harassing email she received.

The response was incredible: BBC News, Buzzfeed, *Guardian*, *Washington Post*, *Nautilus*, *Huffington Post*, *Jezebel*, and many other media outlets wrote about her inspiring project. Even *Backchannel* covered it as late as last month.

Temple-Wood was astonished at the coverage the blog post received. At the time, Temple-Wood was in her final undergraduate semester and had no illusions that her story would extend around the world. "Writing about women scientists seemed like such a special interest, where no one would really care," she says. "Then my life suddenly turned into simultaneously doing a bunch of things—I'd be taking calls from reporters in between classes, labs, shadowing doctors, and trying to get everything together before medical school.

But she is quick to give credit to some of the great projects full of collaborators who are working to address the gender gap on the English Wikipedia, where women only make up 17% of biographies on the world's largest encyclopedia. Temple-Wood helped found WikiProject Women scientists, an effort to ensure that these notable women are well-covered on Wikipedia.

Temple-Wood's friend Rosie Stephenson-Goodknight, who shared the 2016 Wikipedian of the Year Award with her, helped found Women in Red. That project, dedicated to turning "red links" blue by creating articles for women without them, has now created 37,000 articles about women that weren't covered before in English.

That impressive number moves the needle a bit. But did Temple-Wood's editing, even when coupled with the efforts of many other editors, really make a difference in the encyclopedia's coverage about women scientists given the vast expanse of an encyclopedia with 5.4 million articles in English alone?

The answer, one year after the headlines, is an unequivocal *yes*.

Aaron Halfaker, the Wikimedia Foundation's principal research scientist, has been experimenting with new ways to measure content coverage in Wikipedia. "Usually we measure the growth of Wikipedia in numbers of articles, but it's important that we also account for the completeness of those articles," Halfaker argues. "Having a Wikipedia full of half-written articles isn't as valuable as a Wikipedia full of high-quality articles."

He's developed a strategy that uses artificial intelligence to learn from Wikipedians' evaluations of quality, filling in the blanks between manual evaluations (see related report about the modeling strategy). "The result is that we can see clear trends how and where Wikipedia is growing in quantity and quality," he says.

When Halfaker has compared the growth of articles about women scientists to the rest of the encyclopedia, he discovered a striking trend: You can clearly see a content coverage gap for articles about women scientists grow from mid-2002 until 2013. During that decade, articles about women in science were falling behind the rest of the encyclopedia.

Then Temple-Wood and a plethora of collaborators formed projects and started work, and we see a sudden and abrupt shift. By 2014, they had completely closed the gap, and they didn't stop there— . . . the quality of articles about women scientists is about a half-step *above* the quality of the rest of the encyclopedia, and this trend isn't showing any sign of slowing down.

For Temple-Wood, whose life is now filled with medical school, WikiProject Women scientists and Women in Red are proofs of concept. "A group of people chipping away, bit by bit, can make a major difference. We got the ball rolling in 2013," she says, and in the intervening years "the percentage of women's biographies has gone from 14 to 17%, an incredible feat."

For those experiencing online harassment like her, Temple-Wood says that there is no way to beat them—but "you can make sure they don't get the better of you, and writing about women scientists is how I do that." As examples of the stubborn hold of sexism, she points out the people who have asked if she had sex with powerful men to get into medical school or be named co-Wikipedian of the Year. "But I'm the one making a difference," she says. "I'm the one leaving a mark. I and all of the other people in these projects are bringing these fascinating and awesome women to light."

Halfaker has termed this difference-making the "Keilana Effect," named after Emily's Wikipedia editor handle. It is not just data; it is evaluative data from artificial intelligence that is making Wikipedia better every day. It measures not just articles, but impact.

What was inspirational on last year's International Women's Day was not just symbolic. It moved the needle in a very real way. One of the many mantras of the Wikimedia movement is "One edit can make a difference."

Emily made a difference, taking resistance to feminism online, and flipping it, judo-like, into a positive that can be measured, proven, and prototyped. That's not symbolic. That's real change.

> "The vision of equality and liberation promoted by radical feminism is still far from being fully realized."

The New Feminist Movement Should Be No Less Disruptive Than the Second Wave

Laura Tanenbaum and Mark Engler

In the following excerpted viewpoint, published just before the historic 2017 women's march in Washington, Laura Tanenbaum and Mark Engler argue that remembering the militant wave of protests fifty years ago will serve today's feminist movement. The authors give advice to women who are making up the current wave of feminism, particularly in response to President Trump, who has declared, "I wouldn't say I'm a feminist." Tanenbaum is associate professor of English at LaGuardia Community College, and a writer who specializes in feminism. Engler is an author and member of the editorial board of Dissent.

As you read, consider the following questions:

1. Why is it ironic that Trump should be elected president?
2. What do the authors mean by "trigger events" that spur demonstrations and social change?
3. What advice do the authors have for today's activists?

"Feminist Organizing After the Women's March: Lessons from the Second Wave", by Laura Tanenbaum and Mark Engler, Dissent Magazine, January 18, 2017. https://wagingnonviolence.org/feature/when-women-revolted/.

Fifty years ago, feminist organizing in the United States entered a vibrant new phase of activity. While pinning down an exact starting date is a controversial endeavor, several major events in the late 1960s heralded the birth of what is often called second-wave feminism. The year 1966 saw the establishment of the National Organization of Women, or NOW, while 1967 featured both the introduction of the Equal Rights Amendment into the Senate and groundbreaking pickets at the *New York Times* opposing sex-segregated job ads. Then, in 1968, protests at the Miss America pageant set off a whirlwind period that marked the movement's most intensive use of direct action. It also announced the existence of radical feminism, a branch of the movement with an agenda and attitude distinct from the organizing of liberal groups such as NOW.

In the decades since, our society has been transformed by feminism. Changes wrought by the movement have afforded new generations the freedom to transgress once-rigid gender roles, and they have provided hundreds of millions of women with opportunities for personal fulfillment, degrees of independence, and professional accomplishment that were routinely denied their forebears. That said, the vision of equality and liberation promoted by radical feminism is still far from being fully realized.

It is no small irony that, in 2017, Donald Trump, the former owner of the Miss USA franchise and an infamous fount of sexist behavior, will become the nation's president.

The elevation of Hillary Clinton to the White House was meant to be a high point for American women. Instead, the 2016 election pointed to the need for a renewed vision of radical feminism—one that goes beyond corporate feminism's focus on the presence of women in executive suites and high political office, and that instead speaks powerfully to women who work multiple jobs for low wages and who may lack adequate health care, decent housing, and affordable childcare.

Many progressives are rightly dismayed at what Trump's presidency might suggest about the persistence of sexism 50 years after the emergence of the women's liberation movement. What will be significant in facing the horrors of the Trump administration will be whether this dismay can be channeled into a revitalized grassroots movement to confront the sexism and racism that Trump embodies, the newly emboldened threat to reproductive rights, and the coming attacks on the social safety net.

The fact that upwards of 100,000 people are expected to attend the Women's March on Washington, taking place the weekend of Trump's inauguration—and that tens of thousands more plan to participate in parallel marches throughout the country—suggests that such a movement can find a energetic base of support. Those organizing this base should draw lessons from the upheaval of 50 years ago—the history of which is too little known, even among progressives.

Looking back at this period of revolt, we can ask: How did it erupt? Why did it end? And what did it accomplish?

Banner Dropping Miss America

On September 7, 1968, nearly 400 members of a group called New York Radical Women famously disrupted the Miss America pageant in Atlantic City. Judith Ford, the former Miss Illinois—who had performed on a trampoline earlier in the competition—was being crowned the new Miss America. Just as she began giving her acceptance speech, the action started. Feminists who had snuck inside the pageant hall unfurled a banner reading "Women's Liberation." Meanwhile, on the boardwalk outside, hundreds of women symbolically deposited "instruments of female torture"— including bras, high heels, mops, and pots and pans—into a large trash bin to express their view that the pageant commodified women for the profit of men. Flo Kennedy, an African-American activist and lawyer who handled legal defense for the women arrested, fought to include the pageant's racism in the protest and arranged for support from a local black-owned resort, which served as a staging ground for the disruption.

The banner drop was broadcast into homes nationwide on live network television. As the protest grabbed national headlines, group member Carol Hanisch declared, "millions of Americans now know there is a Women's Liberation struggle."

It was the start of something significant. Following the Miss America protest, feminists unleashed a series of high-profile demonstrations and guerrilla theater stunts with lasting implications. When considering the movement's use of disruptive protest, the time between September 1968 and August 1970 is particularly noteworthy, marking a two-year period when the movement successfully captured media attention and made women's liberation into a widely recognized phenomenon. Defying expectations of "ladylike" behavior, feminists gave name to forms of sexism and discrimination that had been previously unacknowledged in the mainstream—raising issues ranging from sexual harassment and discriminatory hiring, to sexist media representation and barriers to reproductive freedom, to unequal pay and a lack of publicly supported childcare.

[...]

The intense period of direct action between 1968 and 1970 also had important consequences, and there is good reason to remember the militant and creative wave of protests that commenced five decades prior to today's Women's March on Washington.

While much social movement theory stresses the importance of long-term organizing, scholar Frances Fox Piven has highlighted the critical role of disruptive protest. She argues that relatively short-lived moments of concentrated upheaval have been vital in producing transformative change in US history. "The drama of such events," Piven writes, "combined with the disorder that results, propels new issues to the center of political debate, issues that were previously suppressed by the managers of political parties that depend on welding together majorities."

A variety of other theorists and activists have also recognized the power of what Saul Alinsky protégé Nicholas von Hoffman—in the wake of the 1961 Freedom Rides—dubbed the "moment of

Feminism Is a Class Issue

"I myself have never been able to find out precisely what feminism is: I only know that people call me a feminist whenever I express sentiments that differentiate me from a doormat."

The novelist Rebecca West wrote this nearly 100 years ago. Today women who want to differentiate themselves from doormats face some of the same problems. More than 40 years after women's liberation became part of radical politics it seems incredible that there is still so much confusion and division about what feminism is.

There have been very great changes in women's lives in the past few decades. They include much more openness about sexuality, millions of mothers going out to work, women breaking into new industries and professions, and acceptance that women will work outside the home, have children outside marriage, and have the right to control their own sexuality.

But work and personal life have been distorted by the constraints of capitalism and have fallen far short of liberation. So there is still as much to fight for.

Women have been drawn into the workforce in millions but working in factories, offices, and shops has not led to an improvement in women's lives, far less to liberation. Women suffer exploitation at work as well as still shouldering the double burden of family and childcare.

The talk of glass ceilings and unfairly low bonuses for women bankers misses the point about liberation, which is that it has to be for all working women and not just a tiny number of privileged women.

Although all women suffer oppression and face discrimination, their life experiences are radically different. Women are not united as a sex but are divided on the basis of class. Middle- and upper-class women share in the profits from the exploitative system in which we live and use this benefit to alleviate their own oppression. Working class women are usually the people who cook, clean and provide personal services for these women, receiving low wages and often neglecting their own families to do so.

Capitalist ideology prioritises the family and the subordinate role of women and children within it, while at the same time forcing individual members of the family to sacrifice "family life" because of the pressures of work and migration.

"21st Century Feminism," by Lindsey German, *Socialist Review*, October 2009.

the whirlwind." In these times, the normal rules of incremental campaigning seem to be suspended. Unexpected crises, political scandals or dramatic public actions—such as the Freedom Rides or the Miss America protests—become "trigger events" that capture public attention and spur heightened levels of social movement activity. These, in turn, create the potential for new triggers.

The period of intensive public protest that commenced in 1968 can be seen as just such a whirlwind. Putting feminism on the national agenda in a way it had not been before, it expanded the range of issues around which mainstream groups were willing to campaign. And it fueled a generative moment in which dozens of new groups, publications, and collectives emerged. While liberal advocacy organizations were important in securing some of the landmark legal and political victories of second-wave feminism, and radical consciousness-raising groups and alternative spaces solidified the social and cultural legacy of the movement, each of these approaches benefited in important ways from the surge in protest activity at the end of the 1960s.

[...]

Why Did It End?

The Miss America disruption initiated a concentrated period that, in hindsight, marked the high point for nonviolent direct action in the second-wave feminism—an outburst of protest that was not replicated with the same intensity before or afterward. Confrontational and provocative, these actions were often derided and mocked at the time, yet they were incredibly effective in shifting public discussion and recruiting more activists to the cause. Zaps, disruptions, and occupations between the fall of 1968 and the summer of 1970 went far in creating a whirlwind moment for women's liberation—a period that can be compared to the year following the 1999 Seattle protests for the movement against corporate globalization, the spring of 2006 for the immigrant rights movement, or the fall of 2011 for Occupy Wall Street.

So why did this whirlwind end?

In part, this is simply the nature of disruptive movements. Frances Fox Piven argues that moments of intensive unrest tend to be short lived, as protest movements "burst forth, often quite suddenly and surprisingly," then subside. One factor is simple exhaustion: peak levels of mobilization cannot be sustained forever, and interest from outside parties often drops off over time. In the case of second-wave feminism, the ever fickle mainstream media's move to turn its attention elsewhere dampened the impact of protest. As longtime activist and co-founder of the New York Radical Feminists Ann Snitow explains, "At first there was a sense that things were bursting out everywhere, and it was exhilarating. We were on the cover of every magazine. But then the media turned the lights off when they realized, 'these women who we liked to make fun of are actually serious.'" While concerted organizing continued during the opening years of the 1970s, feminist groups could no longer rely on the press to amplify their efforts.

Another factor is that changing political conditions—often the result of movements securing some initial victories—can cool organizing. Evidence of this pattern can be seen in the second wave: From 1969 to 1973, radicals in Chicago formed the Jane collective, a network that trained activists to perform their own safe but illegal abortions. Members estimated that they performed 11,000 abortions during this time. However, codification of national abortion rights in 1973, with the Supreme Court's decision in *Roe v. Wade*, brought an end to this civil disobedience. Initial movement success also led to backlash, as conservatives began organizing in earnest to block feminist advances.

[...]

Harvesting From Rich Soil

Describing the impact of whirlwind moments in social movements, political scientist Aristide Zolberg writes, "stepped-up participation is like a flood tide which loosens up much of the soil but leaves alluvial deposits in its wake." Although the impact of movement eruptions are not always as directly traceable as those of traditional lobbying campaigns, these outbreaks can go far in shifting the terrain of political debate and opening new opportunities for progress. After they pass, those seeking to institutionalize change can harvest from richer soil.

Alice Echols writes that, by 1970, "talk of women's liberation (or more often, women's lib) was everywhere." This translated into concrete gains. On each of the three demands that provided points of unity between liberals and radicals during the Women's Strike for Equality—abortion rights, equal pay, and free childcare—the early '70s proved to be times of substantial progress.

Coming of age in an era when even contraception was often unavailable to unmarried women, many feminists spoke of the prospect of unplanned pregnancy as a constant fear in their early adult lives and as a galvanizing force for their activism. Thus, securing abortion rights was a pivotal gain of the period. In 1970, the state of New York passed the most progressive abortion law in the country. Wider progress followed in 1973 with the Supreme Court's decision in *Roe v. Wade*, which marked a sea change in reproductive rights.

Feminists also realized significant gains on issues of employment and educational discrimination. In 1972, the Equal Employment Opportunity Act strengthened language in the Civil Rights Act of 1964 that forbade discrimination on the basis of sex. This shift allowed feminists to effectively pressure the Equal Employment Opportunity Commission to take action against employers. Furthermore, the year 1972 saw the expansion of the 1963 Equal Pay Act, as well as the enactment of Title IX, which prohibited discrimination on the basis of sex in any federally funded education program—including sports. As one telling statistic shows, women made up just 20 percent of college undergraduates in 1950, but constituted a majority by 1990.

Childcare was a final issue on which the new political landscape presented important paths to progress. As historian Rosalyn Baxandall has argued, one of the most prominent and inaccurate myths regarding feminists activists of the late 1960s and 1970s was that they were uninterested in or even hostile to mothers and their kids, and therefore unconcerned with issues related to childcare. In fact, childcare was a demand of many early actions, including the *Ladies Home Journal* sit-in. Amid movement pressure, it was also the subject of extensive legislative hearings between 1968 and 1971. These led to the Comprehensive Child Development Act of 1971, a piece of legislation that would have established universal childcare, with centers funded by the federal government. This represented a truly sweeping proposition by today's standards, and it is remarkable to note that the bill passed through both houses of Congress. Unfortunately, it was vetoed by President Nixon, who explicitly objected to its collectivism.

As Nixon's veto indicates, feminists were by no means able to score all the wins they wanted—and the gains they did make would be targets of later conservative backlash. As the 1970s progressed, and the disruptive peak of second-wave feminism receded, liberals had considerably less success on their own than when their radical flank was most visible. Just three years after Roe, the abortion rights movement suffered a major defeat with the passage of the Hyde amendment, which prohibited the use of Medicaid funding for abortion and which was later expanded to include further restrictions. On the employment front, the difficulty of proving discrimination claims under existing law made lawsuits by liberal groups a slow, piecemeal effort. The shift by liberals to focusing on the Equal Rights Amendment proved vulnerable to counterattack by conservatives, who successfully prevented it from clearing the high bar required for ratification. Finally, as right-wing legislators became more and more vocal in their opposition to universal childcare, and as the Carter White House proved to be a lukewarm ally, feminist advocates were unable to push beyond their success from earlier in the decade.

Such limits notwithstanding, second-wave feminism had durable offshoots and has left a formidable legacy, particularly compared with other movements that have had intensive peaks and then quickly died out. In addition to legally implemented changes, feminism has brought about myriad social and cultural shifts. The women's health movement, best known for the huge success of the collectively produced *Our Bodies, Ourselves,* was highly effective in challenging the patriarchal treatment of women by their doctors. The proliferation of women's studies programs and feminist scholarship has exposed countless people to women's liberation struggles throughout history—something that would have been unthinkable when early second-wave activists burned their diplomas to showcase the disconnect between their educations and lived experiences. And the movement gave name to problems of domestic violence, sexual harassment, and sexual assault, which were once viewed not as social issues at all, but simply as facts of life.

Not only have later generations of feminists been able to build on this foundation, but activists from the second wave also went on to become key players in advocating for a variety of other causes in the late '70s and the '80s, with feminist perspectives influencing the organizing models and direct action tactics. These include the peace and anti-nuclear movements, campaigns against nuclear power, the Central American solidarity movement, radical environmentalism, and the struggle for LGBT rights. Feminist "zaps," for example, became important models for disruptions by ACT UP during the height of the AIDS crisis.

The coming years promise grave challenges. Yet it is worth remembering that the activists who launched the whirlwind of feminist action in the late 1960s faced sexism that was not only pervasive but almost entirely uncontroversial in mainstream opinion. A revived feminist movement in the Trump era—tasked with confronting historic economic inequality, an openly racist president, and an administration promising policies harmful to the great majority of women—should be no less ambitious, unapologetic and disruptive.

> *"Though discrimination is generally less blatant today, women are still treated unfairly, often due to prejudice and stereotypical thinking,"*

We're Using the Wrong Metaphor for the Obstacles Women Face

Sara Martin

In the following viewpoint Sara Martin argues that things have indeed changed for women, but that the obstacles they still face are not very much like the metaphors we have used to frame them. The author contends that rather than simply crashing through a glass ceiling, women must navigate what she calls a "labyrinth" of detours, dead-ends, and unique paths to success in their careers. She draws on research and experts in the field to offer advice and suggestions for both women and organziations. Martin is a writer and editor in Washington, D.C.

As you read, consider the following questions:

1. What percentage of CEOs of organizations are women?
2. What areas require change in order to increase gender equality in the workplace?
3. What type of detours does the author blame for women's lack of success at work?

It's time to abandon the glass-ceiling metaphor, says Alice Eagly, PhD.

That metaphor implies there is a rigid barrier that blocks women from the top echelons of power, explains Eagly, the Northwestern University psychology department chair known for her research on the psychology of gender.

But with 23 percent of American CEOs of organizations now women, according to the US Bureau of Labor Statistics, that's clearly not what's happening today.

A more accurate metaphor for the obstacles women encounter is a labyrinth- "a series of complexities, detours, dead ends and unusual paths," says Eagly. This labyrinth includes sex discrimination, women's domestic responsibilities and sometimes women's own failure to believe in themselves.

That theory is explained in a book due this fall, *Through the Labyrinth: The Truth about How Women Become Leaders* (Harvard Business School Press), co-written by Eagly and Wellesley College psychology professor Linda Carli, PhD.

Eagly and Carli amassed the research on women's leadership from psychology, economics, communications, management and sociology. Their findings document the hurdles women leaders face and suggest ways they can negotiate them.

"The motivation for the book is to help both men and women understand the dilemma women are placed in," says Carli.

To increase gender equality in the workplace, the authors surmise, change must take place on four levels: the culture, the organization, the family and the individual.

Conflicting Expectations

Though discrimination is generally less blatant today, women are still treated unfairly, often due to prejudice and stereotypical thinking, say the authors. "The stereotype of men is more similar to the stereotype of leaders," explains Eagly. As a result, women may not be seen as "tough enough" or having "what it takes" to perform at the top levels.

When women are in leading roles, people expect them to have the qualities of both leaders and women, but that can require a complex balancing act. If they are too tough, women can be disparaged for being "just like a man," says Eagly. If they take a softer approach, they can be viewed as weak or incompetent.

A case in point is Hillary Clinton. She's skilled, confident, knows politics, but people criticize her for not being warm enough. "People rarely have that expectation for a man," points out Eagly. "Do we worry about John McCain being warm?"

To walk that fine line to leadership, the authors suggest that women blend the characteristic male qualities, such as decisiveness and toughness, with the female qualities of warmth and inclusiveness. In short, a successful woman leader generally shows signs of femininity, while assertively taking charge and demonstrating her competence. She can show her proficiency, for example, by being well-prepared and mastering her job responsibilities. She can reveal her femininity by warmly supporting her colleagues.

Women must also build their social networks to be successful leaders, say the authors. Ironically, even though women are viewed as more social beings, they often have less "social capital" in organizations than men.

"There are always these networks within organizations in which decision-making occurs in informal contexts and women commonly get excluded from them—for example, the guys who play basketball on Friday nights," says Eagly.

And those networks are essential, not only in providing emotional support, but in helping to make deals and ferret out the inside scoop on organizational problems, emerging projects or promotions.

That doesn't mean women need to barge in on the Friday night game, Eagly says. They might instead invite colleagues for coffee or an activity or event of their choice.

"Women have to be assertive, not wait for an invitation and sometimes bend to masculine culture," Eagly advises.

Family Ties

These days, a fast-track career demands long hours that often stretch into evenings and weekends. Since women typically have more domestic responsibilities than men, they are usually the ones to cut back their work hours or abandon their jobs when a couple decides to have children.

"These types of detours make it more difficult for women to reach a position of greater responsibility and power," says Eagly. "It's a major complexity in women's lives that men don't face to as great a degree, typically."

Eagly and Carli fear that many women drop out of employment not fully understanding the costs. Not only is it harder for them to rejoin the work force later, but extensive research suggests that a woman's physical and mental health are better if she has multiple life roles-usually both family and employment.

While emphasizing that there is "no one way" to balance work and family, the authors acknowledge that combining child care and employment makes for a very demanding period of life, yet women should consider sticking with both anyway. "In the long run, women who have multiple roles have greater life satisfaction and greater health, despite the complexity of it," Eagly says.

One of the most interesting findings for the book, says Carli, is research that shows today's employed mother spends as much time on child care as the non-employed mother of 1975. "There's all this pressure on women for being 'bad mothers' for working and not spending enough time with their children," says Carli. "And guess what? They are spending a lot of time with their children and sacrificing personal time to do it."

The authors note another emerging phenomenon: Today's fathers are increasingly involved in child care and worry that they are not doing enough.

"Men are not really doing a huge amount of housework, but they are embracing the child care and are still doing their long hours at work," says Carli.

Self-improvement

New data show that today's women are better educated than ever before, and now surpass men in educational achievement. But even with those gains, says Carli, some women doubt their worth in the workplace.

"They feel they don't deserve success or think, 'I should be happy with what I have,'" she notes. And, because women tend to compare themselves with other women—rather than men—they don't often push for the higher salaries and better job perks that men enjoy.

"More often, women need to think about how men are doing," says Carli. They should measure themselves against men with the same qualifications and gather as much data as they can about typical salary and benefit packages for their line of work, the authors advise.

Women also undermine themselves by not talking up their accomplishments, say the authors. According to the research, that may be because women who tout their successes are seen as lacking "feminine niceness" and their immodesty is frowned upon.

"Women need to be tempered in their entitlement and self-promotion, a challenge men don't even need to think about," says Carli.

To avoid disapproval, a woman can promote herself in more subtle ways, say the authors, by asking others to react to her clearly superior ideas, or, when she is being praised, modestly thanking those who helped her.

It's a tall order, say Eagly and Carli, but it shouldn't all be on women's shoulders.

"Women can't be expected to tear down the labyrinth on their own," says Carli. "Organizations have to reduce barriers that favor men over women, men have to share more fully in domestic responsibilities, and society in general has to have a more open and inclusive understanding of what a good leader is."

Periodical and Internet Sources Bibliography

The following articles have been selected to supplement the diverse views presented in this chapter.

Katie Berrington, "A New Wave of Girl Power," *Vogue UK*, January 23, 2017. http://www.vogue.co.uk/article/the-new-wave-of-feminism

Emma Green, "A Lot Has Changed Since 1992, the 'Year of the Woman.'" *The Atlantic*, September 26, 2013. https://www.theatlantic.com/politics/archive/2013/09/a-lot-has-changed-in-congress-since-1992-the-year-of-the-woman/280046/

Rose Hackman, "How Far We've Come: Older Feminists on the Battles They've Faced—and Won. *The Guardian*, 8 November 2016. https://www.theguardian.com/world/2016/nov/08/feminism-women-stories-voting-for-female-president-hillary-clinton

Emily Hill, "Feminism Is Over, the Battle Is Won. Time to Move On." *The Spectator*, 24 October 2015. https://www.spectator.co.uk/2015/10/the-decline-of-feminism/

Maclean's, "Hillary Clinton, 2008: 18 Million Cracks in the Glass Ceiling. *Maclean's*, June 7, 2016. http://www.macleans.ca/politics/washington/hillary-clinton-2008-18-million-cracks-in-the-hardest-glass-ceiling/

Catherine Maddux, "You've Come a Long Way, Baby. But It's Still a Man's Game." *Voice of America*, June 17, 2016. https://www.voanews.com/a/youve-come-along-way-baby-but-its-still-a-mans-game/3380920.html

Liza Mundy, "The Secret of Women in the Senate." *Politico*, January/February, 2015. https://www.politico.com/magazine/story/2015/01/senate-women-secret-history-113908

Kim Phillips-Fein, "The Two Women's Movements: Feminism Has Been on the March Since the 1970s, but So Has the Conservative Backlash." The Nation, June 1, 2017. https://www.thenation.com/article/two-womens-movements/

Joanna Walters, "Feminist Group Appeals to Second-Wave Activists to Rejoin Cause: "You're Not Done." *The Guardian*, 26 June 2016. https://www.theguardian.com/world/2016/jun/26/veteran-feminists-of-america-baby-boomers-activism-pam-ross

OPPOSING VIEWPOINTS® SERIES

CHAPTER 4

What Is Feminism Today?

Chapter Preface

Feminism today is different than it was in even the second wave, and the authors in this chapter are attempting to grapple with those changes. In recent years, feminism has expanded to include issues that have always intersected with the feminist movement, but have not always been a clear part of the definition of feminism. Class, race, gender identity, marriage equality, and economic justice all find their way into today's conversation about feminism. Perhaps because of the gains of previous generations, today's young women have the luxury (if one can call it that, perhaps "voice" would be a better word), to address a wider array of issues. The movement is no longer predominately organized by and made up of white, middle-class women, nor is it limited to issues that affect them.

These changes have led not only to a redefining of the aims of goals of the movement, but to a questioning of the labels associated with it. Fact is, many of the young women today who are passionately supportive of equality in all its manifestations, are hesitant to call themselves feminists. Others, on the other hand, happily pulled on their pink pussy hats and took on the mantel of the movement—marching proudly alongside older women carrying signs saying "I can't believe we're still having to do this." Sisterhood and solidarity are alive and well, despite confusion at times about what to call the whole thing.

In this final chapter, authors are interested in how the current political climate has energized a generation of feminists. But the viewpoints here do not limit themselves to the ebb and flow of politics; they are very much concerned with deeper social change, how it is to be achieved, and how our definitions and understanding of the movement are central to bringing about that change.

"Feminism isn't about hating men or burning bras. It's about women wanting to be treated like human beings who matter."

Misogyny in the White House Is an Outrage

Jill Richardson

In the following viewpoint, published just before Donald Trump's inauguration, Jill Richardson argues that misogyny has no place in US government, particularly in the White House. The author wonders why the people who fight for women's rights are treated with such scorn by some Trump supporters. She specifically quotes Steve Bannon, who was then an advisor to Trump and head of alt-right website Breitbart News.) Richardson is a journalist and columnist for OtherWords.

As you read, consider the following questions:

1. In what year were US women granted the right to vote?
2. In what year did women win the right to own property?
3. Until what year were married couples legally forbidden the use of birth control?

From his campaign rhetoric to his transition appointments, our next president has placed himself squarely in a conservative movement calling itself the "alt-right." That movement, the *Los Angeles Times* reports, "generally embraces and promotes white nationalism, racism, anti-Semitism, homophobia, transphobia, and misogyny."

As a privileged, white, and heterosexual woman, I've never considered my rights under attack to the same degree as the other groups in that list. But to this incoming bunch, feminism is a dirty word.

For instance, Donald Trump's chief strategist, Steve Bannon—a leading figure in the "alt-right" media—called feminists "a bunch of dykes."

Maybe it's time to review what feminism is, and why it emerged in the first place.

Odds are that most of us have no idea how bad women once had it. And men, before you check out, let me assure you that this is no man-hating screed. I have a hunch we'll be on the same page, actually.

No doubt, you probably know that women couldn't vote until 1920. And that women were once expected to be homemakers instead of pursuing careers. But what else are those uppity women whining about?

For starters, there's the right to own things—like our own bodies.

At the founding of our nation, women were bound by something called "coverture"—the idea that a married woman's legal identity was subsumed under her husband's. He owned property and voted for the both of them. And he had a legal right to her body.

This is what the first feminists opposed. Through their agitating, married women first won the right to own property in 1848. The right to vote followed in 1920, but marital rape wasn't illegal in all 50 states until 1994.

Consider that. Just 22 years ago, a Texas man could still legally rape his wife as often as he chose. How dare those crazy man-hating feminists demand they not be raped!

But wait, there's more.

Until 1970, states only permitted divorce when one of the spouses was found "at fault." Only certain reasons were allowed—and falling out of love wasn't one of them. In much of the country, neither was domestic violence.

Once married to your spouse, you were stuck with them unless they committed adultery, more or less. If your husband beat you, that was your problem.

Women who wished to work were relegated to "women's jobs" like teaching, nursing, and secretarial work, and those jobs paid less than "men's work." With men doing all the science, it took until 1966 for the "discovery" that women actually have orgasms.

Married couples couldn't legally use birth control until 1965. Since abortion was also illegal in much of the country, and since a man could have his way with his wife as he chose, women had no control over the number of children they had. (Unmarried Americans only gained the right to use birth control in 1972.)

Over the last two centuries, those are the issues feminists have fought for. So why does feminism still exist?

Because women still earn less than men for doing the same work. And because our bodies still don't enjoy the full protection of the law. To put a finer point on it, the Stanford rapist served just three months in jail for raping a girl behind a dumpster.

Feminism isn't about hating men or burning bras. It's about women wanting to be treated like human beings who matter.

So when the white nationalist website Breitbart, under the management of Bannon, asked, "Would you rather your child had feminism or cancer?" the correct answer is outrage that such a question is asked at all—or that the one who asked it is allowed anywhere near the White House.

> *"Many of the young women who declare themselves feminists, who sticker over sexist ads or set up new websites and feminist groups, are far from hostile to socialist ideas."*

Feminism Cannot Be Separated from Class
Judith Orr

In the following excerpted viewpoint, Judith Orr explores the intersection of feminism and class. The author argues that oppression can neither be reduced to class, nor separated from it. There are a few culturally specific references to British politics and figures in this selection that may be confusing to many readers. However, it is worth wading through those for Orr's interesting take on modern feminism and the class structure of society, and her call for young feminists to take up the causes of socialism. Orr is a British socialist and author.

As you read, consider the following questions:

1. What does the author say is the fundamental divide that shapes the rest of society?
2. According to the viewpoint, the employment rate for working age women rose from 56 percent in 1971 to what percent in 2008?
3. What is still portrayed as the ultimate aspiration for women, according to the author?

"Marxism and Feminism Today," by Judith Orr, *International Socialism*, June 24, 2010. Reprinted by permission.

Another familiar theme is the concentration on women without reference to class. Inequality and poverty are always acknowledged in these debates, but are usually seen as yet another variant of discrimination and simply a greater burden to be borne by the unfortunate victim. "Sexism doesn't operate in a vacuum, but instead interacts with the multitude of other forces shaping our lives, such as race, class, age, disability, and sexuality."[1]

But class is not just one of a list of discriminations, nor can it be reduced to poverty. It is the fundamental divide that shapes the rest of society. A Marxist view of class does not rely on what people think about their position. It is not defined by their income or even what specific tasks they do in their job. Socialists understand class as an objective and dynamic social relationship. Under capitalism a minority class owns and controls the means of producing and accumulating wealth. The working class only exists inasmuch as it is exploited by this class. The capitalists themselves depend on workers selling their labour power to them and creating a surplus off which they can live, invest in future production, etc. The exploiting class have an interest in the most efficient exploitation of their workforce, whatever their respective genders. The superficial trappings of class, for example what sort of homes we live in, what we wear, the holidays we take, all flow from this fundamental relationship, and these change over time.

Marx described how capitalism, by pulling the working class together in ever larger numbers to collectively produce wealth, had created its own gravedigger. It is a social force with immense potential economic power which when mobilised can challenge the very functioning of the system.

However, capitalism also divides us. It generates divisions of race, gender, sexuality and religion, all of which can weaken the ability of workers to successfully take on their bosses. So there is a contradiction: capitalism unites us into the one social force that has the potential to challenge the system, but it also divides workers, encouraging us to blame migrant workers, Muslims or women for the problems in society. But even the pursuit of day to day demands leads to workers cooperating and organising together, whatever the ideas in their heads. In the words of the old trade union slogan, "United we stand, divided we fall."

There is a crude critique in the new feminist texts of the assertion that class is paramount. This claims that socialists deny the great impact the experience of oppression has on people and their lives and ignores the fact that people across the classes can suffer oppression. But the reality is that you cannot understand the full impact of oppression if you try and look at it in isolation from class.

Of course, oppression cannot be reduced to class. Women in all classes can suffer discrimination merely because they are women. Recent examples of this include the way women ministers in the Labour government were often treated in the media. Here is Rod Liddle in the Spectator:

> So—Harriet Harman, then. Would you? I mean after a few beers obviously, not while you were sober… Would you? I think you wouldn't. I think you have more self-respect, a greater sense of self-worth, no matter how much you've had to drink. I think you'd make your excuses and leave… I think you'd do the same with most of the babes who were once, or are now, on the government front bench.
>
> That's the problem with Caroline Flint's statement that Labour's most senior women were used by the prime minister as "window dressing." I mean, would you dress your window with Jacqui Smith, or Ruth Kelly, or Harriet? If you had a window? You might dress the window with Caroline Flint, who, we should all agree, is as fit as a butcher's dog.[2]

Or there was the media reaction to Jacqui Smith making an early speech as home secretary, the first woman to hold the post, which concentrated on the fact that her cleavage was showing. The *Sun* newspaper used the opportunity to "mark a series of female MPs out of ten for the size of their breasts entitled, 'the best of breastminster.'"[3]

MODERN FEMINISM ISN'T HELPING YOUNG WOMEN

While only 23 percent of American women identify as feminists, 47 percent of millennial women do. Unfortunately, policies supported by modern feminists have proved particularly bad for young women. Many of today's young women struggle with significant student loan debt and have a hard time finding a job that will get them out of mom and dad's basement. About 42 percent of women have more than $30,000 in student loan debt, compared to just 27 percent of men.

This could be a result of the increase we've seen in the number of women pursuing higher levels of learning. But significant student loan defaults among this group indicate that women may not be getting a good return on investment. Women are vastly overrepresented in majors that are known to have low returns on investment, such as gender studies or social work.

Yet the feminist movement encourages more young women to pursue these degrees. Their solution is to advocate for further government assistance through policies such as free public college, loan forgiveness and income-based repayment policies that drag out the life of a loan while doing nothing to put pressure on colleges to keep prices in check.Advocating for policies that force others to bear the consequences of one's decisions, such as loan forgiveness, will not advance the position of women, many of whom don't hold bachelor's degrees (as is the case with many men), and all of whom see their taxes increase as a result.

Feminism used to be about removing the barriers of opportunity for all women. Unfortunately, the ideology has taken a sharp departure from its roots. Instead, modern feminism has become a lobbying group for liberal policies that do little to empower millennial women to climb the ladder of economic opportunity.

Events such as this week's Day Without a Woman don't really help. Women on college campuses should reconsider whether modern feminism is helping advance their position or whether they should pursue their hopes and dreams on their own terms.

"Time for Millennial Women to Reject Campus Feminism," by Mary Clare Amselem, The Heritage Foundation, March 11, 2017.

This misogyny in the world of politics is echoed in the boardroom. Last year Cynthia Carroll, the chief executive of Anglo American in the UK, was subject to a sexist tirade from former Anglo deputy chairman Graham Boustred, 84, who told South Africa's *Business Day* that women bosses were hard to find, "because most women are sexually frustrated. Men are not because they can fall back on call girls. If you have a CEO who is sexually frustrated, she can't act properly."[4]

There is no denying that such treatment is sexist, or that the gender pay gap between the highest paid bankers in the city is a phenomenal 44 percent, or that upper class women are trivialised as trophy wives, or breeding stock for an "heir and spare." All of this is evidence that oppression can cut across class. But class shapes the very real material differences between the experience of oppression suffered by someone like Cynthia Carroll and millions of working class women. This is not just about economic disparity in society, although there will generally be a correlation.

Most importantly, the contradiction missed by much feminist thinking is that women workers suffer oppression and exploitation, but are also part of the social force that gives them potential power to challenge their position.

Feminists can miss this element because they accept two false assumptions: that working class people have no organised power, even if they perhaps did in the past; and women are excluded from the core sections of the working class in any case and so are denied the ability to organise effectively.

Myths

Women's work is dismissed by the new feminist authors as marginal, peripheral or just providing the top up to male wages. In one instance the rise of women working outside the home is said to be "due partly to property prices necessitating two incomes."[5] This is a stunning and mistaken generalisation since the dramatic rise in women working outside the home began in the late 1960s. It also ignores the fact that women have dominated some occupations for generations. In the British textile industry of the 19th century, for example, women made up a significant proportion of the workforce, in some cases over 50 percent.

Walter wrote in 1998, "Yes, women are working more. But they often work on the fringes of the economy—in atypical jobs. Atypical work means part-time, temporary, seasonal employment; assisting relatives; homeworking; and illegal employment."[6] Can almost half the workforce be deemed "atypical"?

When Power argues that work has become feminised, that the supposed precariousness that women have faced in the world of work now affects all workers, she appears to be accepting that women's role in the world of work has always been fragile and temporary. Redfern and Aune assert a similar argument about the neutering of class power when they claim that "affluent nations have become post-industrial, outsourcing industrial and agricultural production to poorer countries."[7] Of course, the impact of the economic crisis does mean that everyone feels more insecure about their jobs and future but it is a dangerous leap of logic to then claim the working class no longer has any power.

What is the reality behind the myths? Women are not on the margins of the workforce. The evidence shows that trends for the overall employment rate of women and men have been converging since 1971. The employment rate of working age men fell from 92 percent in 1971 to 79 percent in 2008, while the rate for working age women rose from 56 percent to 70 percent over the same period.[8]

Nor are women's wages just a top up. Lone parents make up a quarter of all families and 90 percent of lone parents are women. Even in families with two parents working, women's income is significant. Women's income represents over half the family income in 21 percent of all working couples.[9]

Even when women have children they are not automatically thrown into a vortex of instability and marginal work. A recent Labour Force Survey shows that for women with children under one, the mean length of time they have been with their current employer is over six years.

Also a recent survey by the Department of Work and Pensions shows that since 2002 there has been a dramatic rise in women returning to the same employer after maternity leave. In 2002, 41 percent moved to a new employer, whereas in 2007 only 14 percent did. Staying with the same employer can mean retaining precious pay and skill levels that many women are forced to forego after having children.[10] It's true that the majority of part-time workers are women, but it doesn't automatically follow that these part-time jobs are precarious.

We can and should complain about some of the sexist airline ads which virtually imply that the female cabin crew will be a businessman's sex slave for the duration of his flight. But isn't it significant that, whatever the advertising clichés, the reality is these very same women have the power to bring an airline company like British Airways to a halt when they decide to strike alongside their male colleagues? These are women for whom mimicking a sexist stereotype unchanged since the 1950s and wearing makeup and high heels is part of their job description.

Disputes like BA and the recent PCS strikes by civil service and other public sector workers show women are and can be organised and are playing a leading role:

> Females had higher union densities in 2009 than males in all occupations except administrative and secretarial, skilled trades, operatives and elementary occupations... For UK employees, male membership in 2009 fell by 157,000 compared with 2008 but only by 6,000 for females over the same period.[11]

Eisenstein shows similar trends in the US, albeit within the much smaller proportion of trade union members there: "Even as the nation's unionisation rate has declined, the female share of union membership has expanded rapidly. In 2004, 43 percent of all the nation's union members were women—a record high." One writer suggests such figures meant that "with close to 7 million women covered by union contracts, organised labour arguably is the largest working women's movement in the country."[12]

[...]

The Family Today

Today, although the majority of women are not solely dedicated to giving birth and raising children, the role of the family still has enormous economic and ideological benefits for the system: economic because individual families undertake the entire costs of bring up the next generation; ideological because families are encouraged to see themselves as atomised, self-contained units where, if you are poor or unemployed, you blame yourself rather than racism in society, economic crisis or education cuts.

The family is also seen by many as a haven from a brutal world that otherwise treats each of us as a mere cog in the impersonal system. The family can be the one place where we can expect and receive unconditional love and support. Family life is eulogised in the media, advertising and popular culture. References to "hardworking families" were a constant refrain during the general election from politicians of all the main parties.

Marriage is still portrayed as the ultimate aspiration for women. Despite generations of women being a part of the workforce, the home is still assumed to be the woman's sphere. It is she who must juggle work, shopping, housework and childcare in order to fulfill society's (and often her own) expectations of her "natural" role. This leads to women often accepting low paid or part-time jobs that fit round school hours and holidays, for example.

At all times the state supports and reinforces this "traditional" view of gender division, with men also expected to fulfill expectations of being the provider. The Tories want to offer tax breaks for couples who marry because they are worried by the trend of people rejecting compliance with the traditional family unit. Women have children later than ever before. Some choose to remain childless. Since the 1970s there has been a fall in the proportion of babies born to women aged under 25 in England and Wales, from 47 percent (369,600 live births) in 1971 to 25 percent (180,700 live births) in 2008.[13]

While traditional ideas about the family do not fit the reality of society today, their resilience reflects the fact that it has survived as a dominant social structure, despite many profound changes in how we live and work. It serves an important purpose in maintaining and justifying the status quo. This is the material bedrock for the ideas about women that permeate society.

Fighting for Women's Liberation Now

Socialists need to start from what unites us with newly politicised women identifying with feminism—their rejection of sexism and anger at injustice and discrimination, and a willingness to fight. We can win a new generation to revolutionary socialism, but not by shrilly denouncing feminism.

We will also do such women a disservice if we merely argue for a different brand of feminism—a socialist or Marxist feminism, for example. Our view of the world and the fundamental revolutionary change we are fighting for are more than one particular approach to fighting for women's rights. We fight against women's oppression in its every expression but believe that socialist revolution is the only way that genuine women's liberation will be achieved.

[...]

Today capitalism is in a prolonged and deep crisis, with brutal wars a permanent feature and climate change posing a threat to the very survival of our planet. Millions in Britain feel a profound sense of anxiety about the future and there is no sense of possibility that the system can deliver a more equal and fulfilled life for ordinary people. The impact of the unbridled market in the name of neoliberalism has ripped away any illusions that collective provision for the vulnerable in society can be expected any longer.

The argument that we need to challenge the capitalist system itself is a popular one. Many of the young women who declare themselves feminists, who sticker over sexist ads or set up new websites and feminist groups, are far from hostile to socialist ideas.

We need to join together with such women in the struggles we face, whether it's against cuts in education or the Tories' potential attempts to attack abortion rights. We should organise debates and protests about sexist advertising and about the fight for genuine sexual liberation. We must be part of every fight against the manifestations of women's oppression but all the time with a vision of how we can win a society free from oppression altogether.

Notes

1. Banyard, 2010, p206.

2. Rod Liddle, *Spectator*, 8 August 2009.

3. Walter, 2010, pp121-122.

4. *Guardian*, 9 July 2009.

5. Redfern and Aune, 2010, p124.

6. Walter, 1998, p23.

7. Redfern and Aune, 2010, p113.

8. BIS, 2010, p10.

9. TUC, 2009, p4.

10. BIS, 2010, p15.

11. http://stats.bis.gov.uk/UKSA/tu/TUM2009.pdf

12. Quoted in Eisenstein, 2009, p216.

13: ONS, 2009, p3.

> "Issues which were central to our
> fight remain intractable, confronting
> younger women all over again."

Feminism's Battle Lines Have Shifted, But Not Changed That Much

Amanda Sebestyen

In the following viewpoint Amanda Sebestyen gives a fascinating, "on the street" glimpse of life in the UK in the early days of feminism's second wave, when women were far less "liberated" than they are today. The author argues that in many ways today's attitudes and policies harken back to that period. Sebestyen calls herself a "grandmother" of the feminist movement and says that her generation can and should lend their voices and experience to the newest phase of the movement to ensure that progress continues to be made. Sebestyen is a journalist, activist, and feminist based in the UK.

As you read, consider the following questions:

1. In what year did the author finally see women dining out alone or with other women?
2. What distinct contributions does the author think that older feminists have to make to the current movement?
3. What is the Tendencies in the Movement as created by the author?

"Focus: The Difference Between Feminism and Women's Liberation," by Amanda Sebestyen, Discover Society, March 1, 2016. Reprinted by permission.

The women's liberation movement has always been rumbustious, cantankerous and full of vehement dissension. It's the other side of that fighting, self-searching, Utopian character we need in order to imagine that we could change the world.

It may be hard to understand just how feudal the post-war agreement on women's role remained, well into the seemingly radical 1960 and 1970s. As JK Galbraith remarked as late as 1973, women had become a servant class "available, democratically, to almost the entire male population." It certainly felt like that.

Women from other more openly patriarchal societies today may recognise a landscape where over 90% of the female population either were or had been married, where rape in marriage was legal until 1991—lagging behind Russia 1922, Poland 1932, Norway 1971, Italy 1976, Canada 1983, and Ireland in 1990, but just before the USA 1993; where a woman could only open a bank account or take out a mortgage if it was countersigned by a male guarantor (other instances linger on well long past the Sex Discrimination Act of 1975). In the England of 1969 when the women's movement began, I hardly ever saw a young woman unglued from the side of a young man, social life outside the couple was unnoticeable. Single women in bars or hotels were assumed to be in the sex industry and usually barred. We are still living the aftermath of those times with the current outrage over changes to women's pensions in the UK.

Now the appearance of the social landscape has changed almost beyond recognition. Consider the line-up of international male and female leaders marching under the "We are Charlie" banner in Paris, a sight shocking only to a tiny fundamentalist sect whose magazine censored the photograph. Look at the eating places where women can enjoy dining alone or with each other—something I literally never saw until my visit to New York in 1978.

We—feminists—did not only prise apart the stereotypes but started to confront gender itself, leaving a lasting legacy of lesbian and gay equality still being fought around the world . However, an integral system of exploitation does not just go away. For those of us "materialist feminists" who saw unpaid labour as the base and centre of women's oppression, the question was always: what happens to all that work? (Delphy 1970; Delphy and Leonard 1992). Would we fight for equality in an unequal society? This last was a question that often seemed to divide our movement down the middle, with socialist feminists sometimes seeming to say "Not at that price." The radical feminist answer, I felt, was "Yes, but only on the way to something bigger." Unfortunately neither of our maps for the world allowed for the huge changes taking place around us in an opposite direction.

Issues which were central to our fight remain intractable, confronting younger women all over again: childcare, the sex industry, misogynist culture and weaponised humour. The Everyday Sexism site and later book reveal the outrage and hurt of Third Wave working women who believe in empowerment but find themselves enduring a barrage of sex harassment every day. The freshness and naivety of their outrage has given them tremendous grassroots power to record and shame their attackers and make other men pledge to behave better. In this they resemble the First Wave of suffrage feminism with its redemptive aspirations: "We are here not because we are law-breakers; we are here in our efforts to become law-makers," in the words of Emmeline Pankhurst.

But in the Second Wave women's liberation movement we probably did view ourselves as law-breakers: "We are against marriage. Behind every ideology we can see the hierarchy of the sexes. We identify in unpaid domestic work the help that allows both private and state capitalism to survive. We detest the mechanisms of competitiveness and the blackmail exercised in the world by the hegemony of efficiency. We want to put our working capacity at the disposal of a society that is immune to this…" (Lonzi 1970)

Across the world we resisted the pull to "exercise a ruling function" as the only accepted proof that females were good enough: "What is meant by woman's equality is usually her right to share in the exercise of power within society, once it is accepted that she is possessed of the same abilities as man. But in these years women's real experience has brought about a new awareness, setting into motion a process of global devaluation of the male world. We have come to see that at the level of power there is no need for abilities but only for a particularly effective form of alienation… Existing as a woman does not imply participation in male power, but calls into question the very concept of power." (Lonzi 1970)

The current emphasis on equality as a metric—how many women at the top table—is inimical to us second wave feminists and is also baffling the young women making up the Fourth Wave of insurgent feminism. As so often in life, grandmothers and granddaughters may have more in common than mothers and daughters. In the generation which came after us, women now in middle age made an important place in the world. Some who might once have called themselves post-feminist are calling themselves feminists now. They have been part of the move away from that feudal, all-for-love, millennia-long unpaid labouring role for women and into a more gender-equitable neoliberal world where the individual achievement is valued above the collective. Now these women are up against power structures that won't budge, and an underside of slavery, trafficking and exploited migrants without rights; some actually providing domestic labour for feminists with careers, a dilemma Kate Clanchy (2008) explores poetically.

At this point we veterans of a long political movement, based on sharing experiences "from the underneath," can feel we have something to tell the world again.

There's a reason why so many feminists of the UK's Second Wave find themselves identifying with the embattled movement, which Jeremy Corbyn's election has started inside the Labour party. At a time when Social Democracy is in crisis and its core policies in health, housing, education and welfare can only be advocated on platforms categorised as far left, we recognise the avalanche of abuse unleashed against anyone who challenges the structures of accepted power. We have literally been there ourselves. As Roberta Hunter Henderson put it in a recent position paper in the Older Feminist newsletter:

"He [Corbyn] has of course been vilified and ridiculed by most of the media but so were we in the 70s. Feminism is no longer so unacceptable these days, thanks to our resilience and all the equal rights campaigning of recent years. But equal pay is of little comfort to the two women a week murdered by their partners, or trafficked or raped. Our politics is anti-patriarchal and goes deeper than equal rights (progressive though that is). Consciousness raising exposed patriarchal values and we must continue to confront them. The personal is political and the social is also political. Economic growth, as GDP, now has priority over the real needs of citizens who are expected to contribute as 'aspirational' consumers. Wealth creation overrides increasing economic inequality. For my part I feel our first priority should be global: the protection of the planet without which there is no politics. We are part of an international community, part of history. Our relations with other nations should be principled and co-operative while conscious of the effect of past injustices: we create our future but we inherit a past. At home our priority should be the sustainability of the environment, not an ever increasing GDP; community cohesion confronting elitism and financial manipulation; protection for the weakest and most vulnerable; and encouragement and creative space for the young instead of debt and disenfranchisement. Hope not fear, NHS not Trident…"

We, the "grandmothers" should create a space for our collective voice. There is an active Fourth Wave of feminism and a growing protest movement. I believe we are part of both but with a distinctive contribution to make.

For five years, a network called 70s-sisters has been meeting in small groups across the UK to explore what we are experiencing now: ageing, loss, death, pleasures, politics. We have returned to consciousness raising as our central form of activism:

We assume that our feelings are telling us something from which we can learn… that our feelings mean something worth analyzing… that our feelings are saying something political, …

Our feelings will lead us to ideas and then to actions. (Amatniek/ sarachild 1973)

We are impressed with the potency of social media organising among younger feminists but unsure how they provide the same experiences of solidarity. As a young LSE student asked Christine Delphy following a showing of the filmed biography *Je ne suis pas féministe, mais...* on 8 January 2016, "How do we do solidarity now, when the idea of doing a good job precludes solidarity?" Delphy's reply was that "Solidarity is never easy because we have several identities; solidarity is always to be defined in the context of a particular struggle." Inside the film itself she had noted that the most important ideas often came out of informal conversations among a group of women. Our own network is now ready to step out in public, using words and actions to make an impact through "a new Think-and-Do Tank" called the Feminist Forum: "We want to use our political experience to participate in politics now and in the future. We work together on many issues, but each member speaks for herself."

The differences among us are important and can't be smoothed out without destroying a live creative voice. Later feminists have found this too. This is why Finn Mackay's book comes most vividly alive when it enters into the arguments that are dividing feminists today. She is inspired by the Reclaim the Night protests of the 1970s and has done more to revive their spirit in the 21stcentury than any other activist. As we march through 21st century streets to a noticeably less hostile reception than we used to get in the past—and with police permission!—I'm still always touched to see the original list of The 7 Demands of the UK Women's Liberation Movement printed on all the new leaflets. Mackay's treatment of our first wild protests (half Halloween, half Angry Brigade) feels almost reverent. But lists of superlatives fail to communicate that past excitement, and the need to fill in past feminist history feels dutiful. It is in the second part of this book, when McKay deals with the conflicts among feminists which have come out of organising the march, that she really makes important connections.

Her treatment of the Transgender controversy seems to me to be just exemplary, and she also has terrific things to say about Judith Butler. In both cases McKay looks inside her own experience, as well as outwards to building a movement aimed at overthrowing patriarchy—which is the essence of feminism.

I should not have been surprised that I caused the biggest ruck of my life by compiling a mock-academic chart called Tendencies in the Movement in 1978. In more polite form it lived on in Ann Oakley's Subject: Woman. Last June, for a discussion on Feminism Then and Now, I attempted a new sketch of a chart to map the different waves of our movement. Here is an excerpt:

1ST WAVE	2ND WAVE	3RD/4TH WAVE
legal and illegal actions	spontaneous/ illegal protests	authorised protests
critical of marriage	anti marriage	extending marriage to everyone
parliamentary focus	extra-parliamentary action	digital activism
women's rights	women's liberation	women's empowerment
Redemption	Revolution	Equality
targets: restrictions/ dual standards	sex roles/ division of labour	gender itself
unchanged: rape	rape	rape
ongoing: unequal pay	unequal pay	unequal pay

Recently I've been going on to imagine a genealogy of change for social movements, which seems to make sense in the context and experience of our particular surge: Prophets; Rebels; Theorists; Pioneers; Mainstreamers; Professionals; Careerists; Opportunists…

The cycle is never complete of course and a new movement ferments and raises itself up. Arguing fiercely, as always.

> *"Things have changed. Feminism is now less despised because it's more obviously needed."*

The Work Isn't Done

Kristin Aune

In the following viewpoint, Kristin Aune argues that, while a generation of women grew up enjoying the spoils of the feminist movement, they are now realizing that they must continue the fight for women's rights. Many believed they were living in a post-feminist world but the current political climate worldwide has disabused them of that notion. The author claims that, as evidenced by global women's marches and the #metoo and #TimesUp movements, another wave of feminism is happening right now and gaining more supporters. Aune is Senior Research Fellow, Centre for Trust, Peace & Social Relations at Coventry University.

As you read, consider the following questions:

1. What was the first women's voting age in the UK?
2. According to the author, what is the gender pay gap for full time workers in the UK?
3. Who began the #metoo movement according to the viewpoint?

It has been 100 years since women won the right to vote in Britain. More accurately, it's 90 years since young women were able to vote; 2018 actually celebrates 100 years since suffrage was given to women over 30.

Feminism is held up as one of the most successful social movements of the 20th century. But ten years ago, when Catherine Redfern and I were planning our book on reclaiming feminism, some said young people just weren't interested in "the f word" anymore.

Back in the 1990s and early 2000s, young women were portrayed smashing glass ceilings in Louboutin heels, and feminism seemed rather outmoded. Many women thought of themselves as post-feminist, feeling there was no need for feminism, since gender equality had been achieved. But this wasn't really true, and a lot of the fear about calling yourself a feminist came from the negative stereotyping of feminists as bitter "killjoys".

It's Still Needed

Things have changed. Feminism is now less despised because it's more obviously needed. Women in the UK have been living under a regime of austerity since the 2008 economic crisis. They have shouldered 86% of the income loss from changes to the tax and benefits systems since 2010, simply because they are more likely to be welfare recipients in the first place.

Meanwhile, the resurgence of the far right has led to violence and harassment against ethnic minority women, with Muslim women bearing the brunt of virulent Islamophobia. There is a stubborn gender pay gap (now 14% for full-time workers), and women pensioners in the UK face one of the worst gender income gaps in Europe.

The list goes on: gender-based violence is alarmingly high. Crime statistics show that one in four women, and one in seven men aged 16 to 59 have experienced domestic abuse. The most harmful forms of abuse—sexual violence, especially—affect mostly women.

Yet three-quarters of councils have cut funds to domestic violence services due to government budget cuts, and a third of referrals to refuges are now being turned away because of a lack of room.

It's Gaining Popularity

These examples of gender inequality explain why more people are identifying as feminists—especially young women. A 2013 Girlguiding survey found that 35% of girls and young women aged 11 to 21 were happy to call themselves feminists. In 2017, this was the case for 43% of 18 to 34-year-old women, according to a poll by Plan International, or 54% of 18 to 24-year-old women, according to UM London.

Today's feminist movement is more diverse than ever before. Feminism has become more attentive to the wider range of experiences of those oppressed by gender norms and stereotypes, including men, non-binary and trans people.

There's also greater awareness of the way that racism, anti-religious hatred, disablism or homophobia work alongside sexism, creating complex forms of prejudice and oppression. It's not so much that feminism has moved "beyond" sexism. Rather, a wider range of voices is now being counted as feminist. The HeForShe campaign, which encourages men to become advocates for gender equality, and Muslimah Media Watch, a forum where Muslim women critique how they are presented in the media and popular culture, are examples of this.

It's Already Happening

If the current situation has anything positive to show, it's that where there's injustice, there's also resistance. Young people are already challenging the forces feminist author bell hooks calls "white supremacist capitalist patriarchy" with style and skill—they don't need to be told how by older feminists. What's crucial now is to recognise the work they are doing and draw even more people to the cause.

Campaigns such as #TimesUp in the US and #tystnadtagning in Sweden have used the star power of famous actors—many of whom are young women—to draw a line under sexual harassment and abuse in the workplace, across all industries. Yet even worldwide movements can start with the actions of a single person: Alyssa Milano credited activist Tarana Burke with starting the #metoo movement more than ten years ago, based on her experiences as a youth camp director for Brooklyn-based Girls for Gender Equity.

As these examples show, feminist activism takes many forms, from a single person signing a petition, to group protests on local issues such as the campaign to close Yarl's Wood detention centre in Bedfordshire, right through to large-scale actions coordinated by women's organisations, such as Women's March. Feminist acts can be taken through formal political routes. For example, by lobbying a local member of parliament, or by informal means, such as sharing information about a topic on social media or boycotting a company known for exploiting women employees.

Individuals can make a difference by working for a women's charity, becoming a local councillor or calling out sexual harassment wherever they encounter it. Even the conversations we have with our friends in our spare time can be a productive way to raise awareness about sexism.

There is no "right" form of activism and no one issue of greatest importance. A century ago, women's rights activists weren't all fighting for suffrage—some of them were working on other campaigns, such as equal access to university education, or a decent wage for working-class women. Nor did getting the vote solve other instances of gender injustice. So this 100-year anniversary is about much more than just "the vote". Feminism is a movement for gender justice, and it needs to be fought by many different people, in many different ways.

Periodical and Internet Sources Bibliography

The following articles have been selected to supplement the diverse views presented in this chapter.

Cohen, Sascha, "The Day Women Went on Strike." *Time*, August 26, 2015. http://time.com/4008060/women-strike-equality-1970/

Denise Cummins, "Why Millennial Women Don't Want to Call Themselves Feminists." PBS, February 12, 2016. https://www.pbs.org/newshour/economy/column-why-millennial-women-dont-want-to-call-themselves-feminists

Jill Filipovic, "The Year Women Stopped Worrying about Being Nice." *Cosmopolitan*, December 4, 2017. http://www.cosmopolitan.com/politics/a14000947/feminism-2017-donald-trump-women/

Anne Kingston, "Feminism's Radical Turn: Far from Being Dead, the Fight for Equality Has Turned Fierce—and Self-Critical. *Maclean's*, March 8, 2017. http://www.macleans.ca/news/canada/feminisms-radical-turn/

Jessica Megarry, "Why #metoo Is an Impoverished Form of Feminist Activism, Unlikely to Spark Change." October 29, 2017. http://theconversation.com/why-metoo-is-an-impoverished-form-of-feminist-activism-unlikely-to-spark-social-change-86455

Katha Pollitt, "We Are Living Through the Moment When Women Unleash Decades of Pent-Up Anger: Let's Hope There's No Going Back." *The Nation*, January 11, 2018. https://www.thenation.com/article/we-are-living-through-the-moment-when-women-unleash-decades-of-pent-up-anger/

Jennifer Rand, "The Third Wave of Feminism Is Now and It Is Intersectional." *HuffPost*, January 1, 2017. https://www.huffingtonpost.com/entry/the-third-wave-of-feminism-is-now-and-it-is-intersectional_us_586ac501e4b04d7df167d6a8

Caroline Simon, "Not Your Mother's (or Grandmother's) Feminism: How Young Women View the Fight for Equality." *USAToday*, College, March 16, 2017. http://college.usatoday.com/2017/03/16/young-feminism/

Mary Wang, "Gloria Steinem's Advice for the Next Generation of Feminists Is a Must-Read for our Time." *Vogue*, October 13, 2017. https://www.vogue.com/article/gloria-steinem-robin-morgan-festival-albertine-feminist-next-generation

For Further Discussion

Chapter 1

1. In this chapter, Rachel Fudge details the many labels that have attached to feminism. Does the fact that there are so many sub-categories or definitions of feminism render the term meaningless? Or does it give it more vibrancy?
2. Issues relating to women of color and immigrants are often at the forefront of social justice movement. It seems, however, that they have been often overlooked by mainstream feminists over the years. Do you think this is changing? If so, why?
3. Marketing has co-opted feminism to use as a marketing tactic. Is that always a bad thing? Why or why not?

Chapter 2

1. Women struggle for equality in most areas of the work world, but the problem seems to be particularly severe in technology careers. Do you think this will change as your generation moves into the workforce? Why or why not?
2. There is a great deal of bickering about whether or not women make less than men. One issue is that women don't succeed as much in their careers as do men because women take off more time to have children, and care for ill relatives. Do you think there is a solution to this problem? If so, what is it?
3. In the 2016 US presidential election, fifty-two percent of white women voted for Donald Trump, even after he made many clearly misogynist comments. In this chapter Morettini says that one reason is that women are trying to be like men. Do you agree? If so, why would it be only white women who voted this way? Does knowing that only fifty-five percent of white women with college degrees voted for

Trump change your thoughts on this? Does knowing that Morettini is male change your analysis of his argument? Why or why not?

Chapter 3

1. Were you surprised to read about the many rights women did not have as recently as the mid to late twentieth century? Does knowing this change your views about the women's movement, its demands and approaches?
2. One of the authors in this chapter discusses the advent of women's studies programs in universities (in this case in the UK). Do you think these programs have been helpful or necessary to the women's movement? Why or why not?
3. Throughout this volume, the issue of a catch-22 for women—if they are strong, they are often considered too aggressive; if they are quiet, they are considered too weak for the job—has come up again and again. What do you think accounts for this problem? In your opinion, how should women respond to it?

Chapter 4

1. Despite the ups and down and arguments about feminism, many young women today are deeply involved in the battle for women's rights. Do you think this generation— perhaps the fourth wave—will make more progress than previous generations?
2. Many women (young and not) agree with the basic goals of feminism, but are hesitant to call themselves feminists. Why do you think this is the case? Do you think feminism today would be more effective under a different name?
3. Many men consider themselves feminists. What do you think is the role of men in the women's movement?

Organizations to Contact

The editors have compiled the following list of organizations concerned with the issues debated in this book. The descriptions are derived from materials provided by the organizations. All have publications or information available for interested readers. The list was compiled on the date of publication of the present volume; the information provided here may change. Be aware that many organizations take several weeks or longer to respond to inquiries, so allow as much time as possible.

American Association of University Women

1310 L St. NW, Suite 1000
Washington, DC 20005
(202) 785-7700
website: www.aauw.org

The AAUW is America's leading voice in advocating educational equality for women and girls. Since the founding of the organization in 1881, AAUW members have examined and researched the fundamental social, economic, educational, and political issues of the day.

American Civil Liberties Union

125 Broad Street, 18th Floor
New York, NY 10001
(212) 549-2500
website: www.aclu.org

The ACLU works to defend and protect the individual rights and liberties that are guaranteed by the Constitution of the United States, including reproductive rights, employment rights, and voting rights.

American Medical Women's Association

1100 E. Woodfield Rd, Suite 350
Schaumburg, IL 30173
(847) 517-2801
website: www.amwa-doc.org

An organization made up of physicians, residents, medical students, pre-med students, health-care professionals and supporters, the AMWA is dedicated to advancing women in medicine, as well as improving women's health. The AMWA functions at the local, national, and international level to provide and develop leadership, advocacy, expertise, mentoring, and strategic alliances.

Canadian Women's Foundation

133 Richmond Street W. Suite 504
Toronto, Ontario M5H 2L3
(416) 365-1444
website: www.Canadianwomen.org

The Canadian Women's Foundation is a public that focuses on helping women and girls to improve gender equality and economic conditions for everyone. They work with community organizations to address four primary issues: prevention of gender-based violence; women's economic development; girls' empowerment, and inclusive leadership. The CWF's definition of women includes people who identify as women, girls, trans, genderqueer, and gender non-binary.

Feminists for Life

website: www.feministsforlife.org

Feminists for Life is a feminist organization that is dedicated to eliminating the lack of resources and support that lead to women to have abortions. The nonpartisan, nonsectarian non-profit was organized in 1972, and shares the core feminist values of justice, non-discrimination, and nonviolence. Their position is that abortion is a reflection that society has not met the needs of women.

Girls, Inc.

120 Wall Street
New York, New York 10005
website: www.girlsinc.org

Offers research-based programs delivered by trained professionals to aid girls in developing their inherent strengths, and give them the support, encouragement, and information they need to navigate the challenges they face.

National Council of Negro Women

Find a local chapter via the website
website: www.ncnw.org

The NCNW is a coalition of 200 community organizations in thirty-two states. Their mission is to lead, advocate for, and empower women of African descent, their families and communities. The NCNW promotes education with a special focus on science, technology, engineering, and math. In addition to encouraging entrepreneurship and financial literacy, they educate women about good health and HIV/AIDS, and promote civic engagement.

National Council of Women of Canada

PO Box 67099
Ottawa, Ontario K2A 4E4
(613) 712-4419
website: www.ncwcanada.com

Founded in 1893, the NCWC has long been dedicated to improving the lives of women, families, and the community. The organization reflects the diversity of society, and aims to encourage informed political decision-making through research, education, consultation, and cooperation.

National Organization for Women (NOW)

1100 H Street NW, Suite 300
Washington, DC 20005
(202) 628-8669
website: www.Now.org

Founded in 1966, the National Organization for Women is a grassroots arm of the women's movement. NOW is dedicated to many issues and many approaches to fighting for women's rights. It has hundreds of chapters, some in all fifty states, and hundreds of thousands of members, many of whom are dedicated activists for the cause of women's rights.

Planned Parenthood

123 William Street, 10th Floor
New York, NY 10038
(800) 430-4907
website: www.plannedparenthood.org

Planned Parenthood provides women's health care, sex education, and information to millions of people worldwide. They are a global partner helping similar organizations around the world.

Bibliography of Books

Margaret Atwood. *The Handmaid's Tale*. (Originally published 1986.) New York, NY: Houghton Mifflin Harcourt, 2017.

Laura Barcella. *Fight Like a Girl: 50 Feminists Who Changed the World*. San Francisco, CA: Zest, 2016.

Simone de Beauvoir. *The Second Sex*. (Originally published 1949.) New York, NY; Knopf, 2009.

Chimamanda Ngozi Adichie. *We Should All Be Feminists*. New York, NY: Random House, 2014.

Jessa Crispin. *Why I Am Not a Feminist: A Feminist Manifesto*. Brooklyn, NY: Melville House, 2017.

Mary Evans. *Feminism*. Thousand Oaks, CA: Sage Reference, 2016.

Betty Friedan. *The Feminine Mystique (50th Anniversary Edition)*. New York, NY: Norton, 2013.

June Hannam. *Feminism*. New York: Taylor and Francis, 2016.

Kelly Jensen, ed. *Here We Are: 44 Voices Write Draw and Speak About Feminism for the Real World*. New York, NY: Algonquin, 2017.

Jill Keppeler. *Women's Suffrage Movement*. New York, NY: Rosen Publishing Group, 2017.

Samhita Mukhopadhyay and Kate Harding, eds. *Feminism, Resistance, and Revolution in Trump's America*. New York, NY: Picador, 2017.

Barbara Molony and Jennifer Nelson. *Women's Activism and "Second Wave" Feminism: Transnational Histories*. London, UK: Bloomsbury Academic, 2017.

Julie Murphy, et al. *Our Stories, Our Voices: 21 YA Authors Get Real About Injustice, Empowerment, and Growing Up Female in America*. New York, NY: Simon & Schuster, 2018.

Deborah L. Rhode. *What Women Want: An Agenda for the Women's Movement*. New York, NY: Oxford University Press, 2017.

Barbara Seaman and Laura Eldridge. *Voices of the Women's Health Movement*. New York, NY: Seven Stories Press, 2012.

Jessica Valenti. *Full Frontal Feminism: A Young Woman's Guide to Why Feminism Matters* (Second Edition). Berkeley, CA: Seal Press, 2014.

Index